DEATH OR DISHONOUR

The world and weapons of the duellist

Frederick Wilkinson

KEN TROTMAN PUBLISHING

Published in 2013 by Ken Trotman Publishing.
Booksellers & Publishers
P.O. Box 505
Godmanchester
Huntingdon PE29 2XW
England
Tel: 01480 454292
Fax: 01480 384651
www.kentrotman.com

Design by
Stephen Summerfield

Printed in Great Britain by the MPG Books Group, Bodmin and King's Lynn

ISBN: 978-1-907417-37-5

Contents

Contents 3

Acknowledgements 4

Chapter 1: A Deadly Choice 5

Chapter 2: The Seconds 21

Chapter 3: The Pistols 27

    Locks 27

    The Stock 32

    The barrel 35

    Cases 38

    The advent of percussion 43

Chapter 4: Duelling in decline 45

Chapter 5 Duelling abroad 47

Chapter 6 The Gunmakers 49

    A Selection of Makers 51

Bibliography..52

Examples of Duelling Pistols 53

Acknowledgements

The author and publishers are extremely indebted to Thomas Del Mar for his kind permission to use so many illustrations. These remain the copyright of Thomas Del Mar ltd.

They also express their thanks to Chapel Bay Fort Museum for permission to use the illustrations as noted in the text.

Chapter 1:
A Deadly Choice

Who steals my purse steals trash; 'tis something, nothing
T'was mine, 'tis his, and has been slave to thousands;
But he who filches from me my good name,
Robs me of that which not enriches him,
And makes me poor indeed.

Iago's speech from Shakespeare's *Othello* sums up the essence of the concept of duelling. The 'good name' is valued above property and money and the phrase could be changed to honour, respect or self-esteem but it would still be no easier to define precisely what is meant. It suggests that what people think of a person is of enormous value. Despite its ephemeral nature this vague concept has been responsible for the death of hundreds, indeed thousands, of people over the ages. Even today with the scourge of city gang-culture, disrespect - another way of defining the situation - often leads to violence and murder. This lack of respect can be perceived in a side-glance, a tone of voice, a casual comment or even a gesture, all of which were totally innocent of any deep significance

An associated problem in understanding the concept of honour is that it is so individual that what, to one person, is a harmless, joking remark or innocent comment can be, to another, a deeply insulting, disparaging slur. Similarly a lack of courtesy or an inconsiderate action could produce the same disastrous outcome. *The Times* of March 19th 1792 carried a report of a duel fought in Ireland between a Mathew Yelverton and a Mr. Johnson in which a brace of pistols was fired by both principals. Yelverton was hit in the right thigh by two balls *within an inch of each other* but the bullets were extracted and *no danger is apprehended*. The cause of this affair was that Mr. Johnson had made use of a coach previously engaged by Mr. Yelverton.

In the past, when it was felt that an insult was perceived and called for a response, there were, for centuries, only two possible resolutions to the situation - a duel or an apology. The situation was made even more complex because the giving of an apology might be seen to be demeaning to the giver's honour. In any case at certain periods an apology was not even to be considered and there were, in some codes of duelling, certain insults which were so serious that an apology was totally unacceptable.

If an apology was demanded but was not forthcoming then a formal, more or less obligatory, series of prescribed steps were set in motion which could well culminate in the death of one or both participants. Over the centuries this routine has varied in detail but the basic procedure remained unchanged with the very important first step being the appointment of friends to act as seconds. Once appointed it was they who took over preparations for the duel and dealt with any communication between the duellists. The seconds set the place of the duel, the date, the time, the conditions of the combat and they supervised the choice of weapons. When the duel took place the seconds were expected to oversee the event and ensure that the principals kept strictly to the rules. Accepting the position of a second was not a task to be undertaken lightly for, by English law, if there was a fatal outcome to the duel the seconds were deemed to be just as responsible as the duellist and faced a charge of murder.

The concept of maintaining one's honour or integrity by risking life or limb may be traced back to the earlier trial-by-ordeal when guilt or innocence might be decided by some physical reaction by, or of, the body. The form of ordeal varied over the ages but was based on the concept that God, or some supernatural power, would intervene to expose the guilty and protect the innocent. One of the earliest forms of ordeal was the use of water; the two people involved in the case were immersed in a river or pond which, it was believed, would reject the guilty person and he would then float whilst the innocent would sink.

In another scenario the accused had to hold a hot iron in the bare hand for a set time when the innocent would show a less serious wound than that of the guilty. Yet another method involved plunging the hand into boiling water. In trial by combat, introduced into Britain by the Normans, it was thought that god would guide the weapon of the innocent and deflect that of the guilty. In this particular style of ordeal there were certain safeguards so that an accused woman or man incapable of fighting could be represented by a champion. In March 1163 Robert of Monthert accused Henry of Essex of cowardice in battle. The combat took place on an island in the Thames and the loser, Essex, was deemed to be guilty and was outlawed and had all his estates confiscated. He was lucky in that he survived the combat and became a monk[1].

The Second Pofition of the Difarm after having parried the Thruft in Tierce.
Publifhd as the Act directs Aug.st 1785

A page from an illustrated book by Mr Angelo of London in 1787 demonstrating one of the many thrusts and parries with the small sword.

---

[1] *Jocelin of Brakeland Chronicle*, Nelson Medieval Text p68

Over the ages the concept of personal combat to prove ones integrity, the duel, became formalised and rules were created with one constant, basic concept which was that each duellist should have an equal chance of surviving. The choice of weapons was obviously one vital consideration and in this interest of equality it was important that both weapons should, as far as possible, be identical. When edged weapons were most used in duels, since a slightly longer blade might make a real difference, this equality was easier to ensure for it was a simple matter to measure the weapons.

The importance placed on this feature is seen in a case reported at the Old Bailey[2] on the 16th May 1678. Lt. Charles Dalison was run through by a Charles Pamplin who apparently stole and used a *very long sword* which, compared with that of Dalison, *exceeded it a quarter of a yard in length* (9 inches, 22.5 cms.). Despite attempts to defend his action Pamplin was charged, tried, found guilty and sentenced to death[3].

A similar case was that of 12th October 1692 when Henry Tankard was charged with murdering John Burton[4]. The case arose as the result of a duel fought in a field behind Southampton House, in Bloomsbury, central London, apparently over some drinking quarrel. During the subsequent trial a witness stated that he had seen Mr Burton lying on the ground, face down with his sword still in its scabbard beneath him and that he had suffered a five inch wound to his breast. Both swords were produced in court and Mr Tankard was told that his sword was '*a very unlawful one to fight a duel withal, and much longer than Mr. Burton's*'. Unfortunately no more detail was given but a verdict of guilty of murder was returned and Tankard was executed at Tyburn[5] on the 26th October 1692.

---

[2] *The Central Criminal Court London*
[3] *The Proceedings of the Old Bailey* website T16780516
[4] *Trial* t16921012-1
[5] Tyburn, near the present Marble Arch in London, was the site of the gallows where public executions were carried out until the 18th century.

A particularly fine German swept-hilt rapier with a blade from Toledo, the Spanish town noted for the quality of its swords. [Thomas Del Mar]

For centuries swords were part of a gentleman's costume and by the 16th century the long, heavy, bladed weapon had evolved into the elegant rapier. This was a thrusting weapon as opposed to the essentially slashing blade of earlier times. The blade was long, narrow and usually stiff and had a hilt composed of a metal cup or a series of intertwined bars of various shapes designed to protect the sword hand. The conversion to a thrust, rather than a cutting style of combat, led to the development of new styles of sword-play or fencing and schools were established by experts, masters-of-fence, for the teaching of these new techniques and illustrated instruction books were published. The rapier was normally carried in a sheath of leather-covered wood suspended from a waist belt and supported by a decorative hanger. The weapon was subject to some legal regulation and in 1557 Elizabeth I decreed that no sword or rapier was to have a blade *above the length of a yard and a half-quarter* [6]. It is interesting to speculate on how firmly such a decree was enforced.

One popular variant of combat was with the sword in the right hand and a dagger in the left hand but there were others styles which involved the use of a cloak, a small circular shield or buckler or, strangely, a lantern. Basic fighting techniques were expanded and a variety of styles evolved and in the 17th and 18th centuries it behoved any man with pretensions to quality or social status to master these techniques for there was an ever present chance of a remark or some misunderstood action leading to the issue of a challenge.

During the 17th century the rapier was gradually abandoned and by the eighteenth century had been generally replaced by a shorter, lighter, less elaborate, but often finely decorated, small-sword. The hilt was decorative, often of silver, whilst the blade might be flat or hollow ground and on some swords the upper section, below the hilt, was wider than the rest of the blade. The small-sword was also a thrusting, rather than slashing, blade and as before, schools were established to teach its use. Fencing or sword-play became a normal part of a young man's social skills. However by the 1780s and 90s the fashion of gentlemen carrying swords had rather fallen from favour and as this became less commonplace there was a corresponding decline in its use in duels.

From their appearance in the 14th century, firearms gradually became more effective and more common and by the 18th century many types of pistols were readily available. This trend, coupled with the gradual abandonment of the fashion of wearing swords, was reflected in the increased use pistols in the duel. In Great Britain, until the late 19th century, there were virtually no legal restrictions, except for religious grounds, on the possession of firearms for they were not seen as a potential threat. Gun making was accepted as a respectable and profitable trade and there were many gunmakers, famous and obscure, based in London. Most towns boasted several provincial

---

[6] A yard was 36 ins and a half quarter or one eighth was 4 ½ ins making a total of 40 ½ inches or 1m 16.5cms.

makers and vendors, many of whom had their names engraved on pistols which were in fact purchased from gunmakers in Birmingham and London.

This change of weapons in the duel may have had some affect on the chances of a duellist surviving the ordeal. The techniques involved in firing a pistol were far less complex and easier to acquire than mastering a style of fence. It was so much simpler to practise with a pistol when any open space could suffice as a shooting ground and many gunmakers of the period had some form of range attached to, or incorporated into, their shop and were no doubt very ready to offer advice and coaching. There was a counter-balancing factor in that a wound from a bullet, rather than a sword cut, was more likely to lead to infection. The blade was usually clean and would be withdrawn from the wound as soon as it was inflicted, whereas the lead bullet might well become imbedded in the body. As the ball penetrated the flesh it almost certainly carried into the wound particles of clothing, fouling from the pistol or the mould and any other dirt, all of which could easily lead to infection. Extracting a bullet from a wound was not an easy task and was very painful, without anaesthetics, certainly adding to the risks and suffering of the victim.

Prior to the later part of the eighteenth century it seems that any pistol might be used in the duel but as the protocols of duelling developed it became a requirement that both opponents had to have, as far as possible, identical weapons. The use of ordinary pistols was now considered inappropriate and naturally gunmakers were only too ready to supply pairs of pistols. Pairs of pistols had been in common production for centuries but now the idea of supplying the pistols complete with accessories in a specially made case was the fashion. A cased pair of specially designed, identical, duelling pistols was expensive but the cost was probably seen as a necessary expense for something essential for the owner's social status.

From the 17th century the whole ritual of the duel became prescribed and although it specified that the pistols should be as nearly identical as possible on occasions this was not the case. This is apparent from the London trial held on the 5th June 1782[7] that involved Bennet Allen, a clergyman of reasonable wealth for he had a salary in the United States of America of a thousand pounds a year. Appearing with him was Robert Morris and both were charged with killing Lloyd Dulany in a duel. The origin of this fracas was an article which had appeared in 1775 in *The Morning Post*, a newspaper published in Maryland, United States of America. The article contained some disparaging remarks about the brother of Lloyd Dulany who immediately published a repudiation of what he regarded as slurs but this evoked no response or admission from the anonymous writer of the original article. In 1779 the first article was followed by another in which Lloyd accused the unknown writer of being *a coward, a liar and an assassin.*

Nothing further transpired until seven years later when, on Tuesday 18th June 1782, a Mr. Allen arrived at the home of Mr Dulany who was then living in London. Lloyd was not at home but Allen apparently left a letter in which he admitted he was the author of the article and presumably, demanded an apology or satisfaction over Dulany's derogatory comments. When Dulany arrived home and read the letter he became very upset and apparently decided that he would fight Allen as soon as possible. He immediately arranged for two friends, Morris and Delaney, to act as seconds and since only Morris was later put on trial it may be assumed that Delaney was acting for Dulany.

Dulany was determined to settle the matter as soon as possible and borrowed some pistols from a friend who, during the later trial, pointed out that Delany had never seen them before. Allen had his own pistols but it was then realised that they had no balls with which to load his pistols. All four took a coach and went immediately to the Haymarket to the shop of Robert Wogdon, a famous gunmaker who had acquired a reputation as a supplier of duelling pistols. When they arrived Wogdon told them that he had none of the correct size of balls in stock. This raises an interesting question as to what calibre were Allen's pistols since one might well expect that Wogdon, a leading gunmaker, would have had available a stock of balls for most of the usual calibres.

---

[7] Trial t17820605-1

He agreed to cast some balls which he did and then loaded Allen's pistols. Delancey, acting as Dulany's second, refused an invitation, as was his right, to watch the loading because he felt that this should only take place at the agreed site as stated in the rules of duelling. Robert Wogdon was subsequently called to give evidence during the trial and stated that it had taken him six minutes to cast the balls. He described the loading and said that he used one charge of powder and one ball - *the usual charge I give when I sell them*[8]. He also explained that he had put *a piece of leather about the ball.* He confirmed that the pistols were smooth bored in which case it was perhaps a little unusual to patch the balls, a practice normally only recommended when loading rifled pistols. During the trial the pistol used was valued at five shillings suggesting that it was not, in any way, special or unusual.

Despite the fact that it was now getting dark all four adjourned to Grosvenor Gate in Hyde Park, Central London, where Delancey proposed that the shooters should fire at a range of twelve yards. This suggestion was rejected as Allen's second, who thought this too far, suggested eight yards. Dulany agreed and the two principals took up their position and then the signal to fire was given by the seconds removing and waving their hats. The duellists fired and Delancy fell mortally wounded and died on the following Friday 21st.

At the trial the evidence revealed some minor anomalies for Delancey stated that Dulany's pistols, which were apparently borrowed, were *screw-barrelled* and Allen's were *plain.* The expression screw-barrelled is normally taken to mean that the barrels were rifled whereas Allen's were smooth bore. Most duelling rules of this period denied the use of rifled pistols since they were generally more accurate and more powerful than smooth bores. Delancy also thought Allen's had slightly longer barrels but at short ranges this may have had no real bearing. Allen's ball penetrated his opponent's body, piercing the lungs and finished up under the left shoulder. The resting place of the fatal bullet is consistent with the shooter taking the normal stance of the duellist, standing sideways-on presenting his right side to his opponent. The surgeon who dealt with the wound described it as being three inches

---

[8] This might suggest that Wogdon sold his pistols ready loaded lacking only the priming.

long and half an inch deep suggesting a fair sized ball which he had duly extracted.

Evidence was given that Allen had been practising his marksmanship in the garden of the house where he was staying, by firing at a target with his pistol. He was said to have fired as many as thirty shots, although one witness thought only twelve. This suggests that Allen had very obviously been preparing for the duel and was therefore likely to have been a more proficient shot. It also raises an interesting query as where he got his supply of bullets. Did he have a stock or had he cast them himself and if so why did he not have any ready for the duel?

In his evidence he claimed the priming flash had blinded him and he could not see his opponent clearly. Character witnesses were called for all those involved and the judge summed up the evidence, reminding the jury that, if some one was killed as the result of a duel, it became a case of murder and the second supporting the duellist was as culpable as the duellist. There may have been some slight discrepancies over details of the case but it took the jury only a quarter of an hour to find Allen not guilty of murder but guilty of manslaughter and Morris, the second, not guilty. In his judgement the judge condemned duelling but accepted that Allen was *well regarded* and sentenced him to be fined one shilling (roughly equivalent today to £3) and imprisoned him for six months in Newgate[9].

The passage of time often strengthened rather than weakened the desire for satisfaction. The above case, fought in 1782, had its origin in 1775 and long periods between incident and duel were not so unusual. A duel fought in Hyde Park September 1787 had its origin in Bengal, India; in 1785 when a Major Browne received what he thought was a rather peremptory order from the Governor General Sir John Macpherson. Browne felt that in the circumstances he could not demand immediate satisfaction but later when both were in England a challenge was issued and accepted. It was nearly fatal for Sir John as one of his pistols misfired and two rounds were fired, one ball passed through his coat near his left breast and the second struck

---

[9] The main criminal prison in London and notorious for the terrible conditions.

his pocket book and the duel finished with a reconciliation and *without injury to either party.*

The sentence passed on Allen (see above) was not unusual and a similar one was handed down in the case of Richard England heard on 17th February 1796[10]. He was charged with the full, formal, legal language intended to present a charge that could not be contested in any minor detail; that *on the 18th June in the twenty-fourth year of his Majesty's reign, (1784) with force and arms, in and upon William Peter Lee Rowolls, feloniously, wilfully and of his malice aforethought, did make an assault; and that he; a certain pistol, value 5s[11] charged with gunpowder and one leaden bullet, which he in his right-hand, then and there held, feloniously, wilfully and of his malice aforethought, did shoot off, at, against, and upon, the said William Peter Lees Rowolls; and that he, with the leaden bullet aforesaid, out of the said pistol, by the force of the gunpowder aforesaid, by him discharged and that as aforesaid, thereupon feloniously, wilfully, and of his malice aforethought, did, strike, penetrate, and wound him the said William Peter Lees Rowolls, in and upon the right side of his belly, near his right hip, thereby giving to the said William Peter Lees Rowolls a mortal wound, of the depth of four inches, and of the breadth of half an inch, of which he instantly died; and so the Jurors for our Lord the King, say, the said William Peter Lees Rowolls, the said Richard England feloniously, wilfully, and of his malice aforethought, did kill and murder, in manner and form aforesaid.. He is also stood charged with the like murder upon the Coroner's Inquisition[12].*

The Prosecutor stressed that if a duel resulted in the death of another person it was legally murder, no matter what the cause. The original quarrel had been over some gaming debts at Ascot races in 1780 but in February 1784 the situation was exacerbated by Mr England who made some derogatory remarks about Rowolls being in debt. The outcome was a challenge resulting in a duel which took place at Cranford Bridge.

---

[10] t 17906217

[11] Five shillings is the equivalent of current money £14.

[12] Every unexpected death had to be placed before a Coroner who, with a jury, decided on the circumstances.

Amazingly four or five shots were exchanged with no result but after reloading, apparently Rowolls' pistol, either deliberately or by accident was discharged and the shot hit the ground just in front of him and England then discharged his pistol harmlessly in the air. Despite all of this which could have ended the affair without disgrace the stubborn principals refused to reconcile their differences and the pistols were reloaded yet again. Rowolls fired and missed but England apparently now took his time in aiming and fired, killing Rowolls. England immediately left the scene and spent years abroad and was officially outlawed. He eventually returned to England when Rowolls' mother instituted legal proceedings and England was duly arrested and charged with murder.

At his trial one naval officer declined to give evidence least it might place him in danger since he had acted as second to Rowolls. Evidence from eye-witnesses substantiated the sequence of events and also reported that a spectator had exclaimed *Gentleman is not three times enough to try your courage, or do you want to murder one another?* The same witness reported seeing two gentlemen putting their pistols *into a box* suggesting that a cased set of pistols had been used.

The judge summed-up stressing the difference between murder, a capital crime which carried a mandatory death sentence, and manslaughter[13] which did not. The jury apparently had few doubts since it took only twenty five minutes for them to reach the verdict of not guilty of murder but guilty of manslaughter. Passing sentence the judge said that England had forfeited any leniency since he had fled the country for twelve years and he also implied that he thought the verdict was wrong and it was really a case of murder. The judge went on to demonstrate that such cases of manslaughter would attract severe penalties and fined the prisoner one shilling[14] with twelve months imprisonment.

---

[13] Manslaughter is an act which results in death but such an event was not intended.
[14] Equivalent purchasing power today £3.14

Another trial on 14th January 1818 saw three men on trial for murder as they had been involved with a duel resulting in the death of one principal[15]. Evidence was given that all involved, including the unfortunate victim, had expressed regrets and forgiveness and a string of character witnesses testified to their good qualities. The jury found all three guilty of manslaughter with three months imprisonment.

As early as February 1683 there was a case of a second being charged with murder. Christopher Billip was accused of being involved with the death, in a duel, of Mr. Glower in Covent Garden, London. There was some confusion in the evidence which sought to prove that he had been involved but Billip claimed that he had no connection with the duel. The jury evidently believed him as they returned a verdict of not guilty[16].

Although duels involving more than the usual single shot did happen they were unusual but few more so than that of Munro of the 16th Dragoons and Mr. Green which took place in December 1783 at Battersea Fields in London. Firing at a range of six yards they fired three shots, the third hitting Green in the side. Despite pleas from his seconds Green refused to accept the matter as settled unless Munro gave him a public apology, a request rejected. Another two shots were fired and Munro was wounded in the knee but Green received a lethal wound.

The role of second was not without its risks as was shown in the case of Rob. Keon of Dublin in January 1788. Whilst preparing for the duel Keon callously shot his opponent in the head. Mr. Plunkett, his second, exclaimed *A horrid Murder* where upon Keon's brother attempted to shoot him saying *If you don't like it, take that* but fortunately for him the pistol malfunctioned. R.Keon was charged with the murder of George Reynolds, found guilty, sentenced to death and, despite valiant efforts by his lawyers, failed to win a reprieve and was duly hanged in February.[17] Even more unfortunate was the

---

[15] t18180114-39
[16] t16830223-8
[17] *The Hive Vol III No. 73 and 74*

second who stood too close to his principal and was hit and killed in November 1821.

As with everything luck was an unknown quantity as Captain Cuthbert of the Guards was to discover in June 1792. The Captain had been dealing with a riot in the streets of London and issued orders that no carriages be allowed to pass along Mount Street. Lord Lonsdale's coach was duly stopped from driving along the road. He lost patience and shouted at the officer. *You rascal, do you know that I am a peer of the realm?* The Captain replied that *I don't know whether you are a peer, but I know you are a scoundrel, for applying such a term to an officer on duty; and I will make you answer for it.*

The duel took place and a brace of pistols was discharged with no injury to either principal. It was then found that Lord Lonsdale's shot had hit the Captain but had struck a button and so failed to penetrate, at which point the seconds intervened and the affair was settled amicably.

Even deadly duels could evoke a somewhat macabre humour. Two Irish lawyers fell out and were set to fight but one was very thin and the other quite tubby and he complained that his opponent was being given a much easier shot. The thin one then offered to narrow the differences by having his outline chalked on the left side of the other man. He then proposed that only hits within the chalked area would count. Shots were exchanged but no hits were recorded.

Whilst society, in general, perceived the practice of duelling as being acceptable there was slowly growing an opinion that perhaps it was not quite as laudable as some claimed. In October 1786 *The Times* carried a story about a quarrel at Covent Garden Theatre which was expected to lead to a duel. The report commented *That these contests are now become so frequent as to disgrace all propriety and civilisation.*

As early as August 1789 *The Times* newspaper published an article by a writer using *Tireasis* as his pen-name which condemned the duel in no uncertain terms: *To endanger our lives on every trifling dispute is not a sign of true courage, but rather a fanaticism and perfect foolhardiness.*

An early 19th century, popular weekly pocket magazine was *The Web or Weekly Register of Remarkable Events* and issues No 73 and 74 Vol. III contained an article mocking the duel. It expressed the fear that duelling *will never be abolished* but suggested that it is *unchristian, illegal, immoral – and nugatory as to its effects.* The writer said that *As the fashion increases we see beautiful duelling pistols ticketed up even in the pawnbrokers' windows.*

BARNEY fighting a DUEL.

A satirical view of the duel in a cartoon by the famous cartoonist George Cruikshank (1792-1878).

He recounts a story about *a fighting baron* who fearing that *wadding* might enter a wound fought and won a duel whilst naked. He also reports that some duellists practised by using an egg as a target or by snuffing out a candle at twelve paces.

He suggests that reluctant or sympathetic seconds tried to mitigate the results by substituting cork balls, painted to look like lead, for real balls and he also mentions paper-pellets. Another device designed to avoid the possibility of a lethal duel whilst preserving a concept of honour was to ensure that the law became aware of the planned event. Officers would then turn up and stop the duel and take the principals in front of a magistrate who would issue an order forbidding them from taking part in any duel, so providing a perfect excuse for any future refusal to fight.

To curb the duel the writer suggested that the Chancellor of the Exchequer should grant permission for duels to be fought at the well known London site of Chalk Farm on the purchase of a stamped certificate for a fee of £500. Any duellist who failed to pay and then fought would be found guilty and hanged on the top of Primrose Hill, another well known place. The fee would be adjusted to the social status of the principals.

The author feared that even the threat of capital punishment would not deter determined gentlemen and he favoured the efforts of Frederick King of Prussia who, in 1733, decreed that all seconds and principals involved in a duel, even if none was wounded should suffer death and be buried as common criminals. The author concluded his article by saying that he doubted it would ever happen but some form of court of honour would be a far better way to settle problems without bloodshed. His last sentence is a rather cynical comment that the Chinese never fight duels for they have no honour to fight for and *quietly let bribes effect (sic) everything.*

Chapter 2:
The Seconds

Preparations for the deadly meeting were the responsibility of those very important friends of the duellist, their seconds. One of the most comprehensive accounts of their duties is included in a pamphlet, first published in 1824, and entitled *The British Code of Duel* which has a sub-title of *A Reference to the Laws of Honour and the Character of a gentleman.*

The writer begins by attempting to justify the duel by likening it to a state going to war when there is no other course open to it. He basically accepts that death resulting from a duel was legally murder but points out that there was no specific law which prohibited duels and said that action against them was commonly taken on the grounds that they were a breach of the peace. In the late 18th and early 19th centuries it was not uncommon for police officers to be sent to prevent a duel taking place. Despite their efforts duellists sometimes evaded them and were able to fight. This was one reason for the need for the seconds to keep the planned duel as private as possible. The writer also attempts to justify honour and the status of a gentleman, his views clearly expressing the very class-conscious attitudes of the period.

The *Caledonian Mercury* newspaper of 10 March 1802 carries a report of an example of attempted police intervention. It reports that on the morning of the 7th March a duel was fought in Kensington between Lord Camelford and Captain Best of the 48th Regiment in which Camelford was shot through the heart. As the original quarrel took place in public, details of the duel were soon circulating and officers from the Police Offices in Marlborough Street and Bow Street were dispatched to prevent it. They kept watch on the principals' houses but somehow the duellists eluded them with a fatal result.

Such an incident was reported in *The Times* on 21ˢᵗ September 1792, When a son of a cheesemonger sent a challenge to a gentleman at Kensington. The challenged sent two police officers with a Justice's Warrant to arrest the man and take him to Bow Street. He was forced, on a penalty of £100, *to lay bye all weapons of destruction in future*. An exception was made in that he was allowed keep one knife, *his semi-circular one which is a necessary implement of his trade*. The article also comments that *duelling ever gets more and more into disesteem* and some of the feeling generated was that these people were assuming a feature previously reserved for gentlemen.

When an insult, real or imagined, was experienced the sufferer was expected to make a dignified response and from that point on the duellists placed the matter in the hands of their seconds. Protocols defined that they should be of the same social standing as the principals and, preferably, were unmarried. It was possible that they might even be challenged on their suitability to serve as a second and if necessary they had to be able to prove that their social status was appropriate for them to act in this position.

It was they who delivered the challenge and this procedure was defined in detail. When all the niceties of social standing had been settled and the challenge delivered and accepted the next step was to select a suitable site for the duel. The location had to be agreeable to both parties and it was stressed that it *should be away from the haunts of men*. The seconds were expected to arrange for a surgeon to attend and both principals could supply one of their own choice if they so wished but it was quite acceptable for only one surgeon to attend on the understanding that he would, if necessary, treat both duellists.

When the two opponents finally met at the approved site the seconds were duty bound to attempt reconciliation between them but if they failed an inspection process began. The object was to ensure that neither duellist had any hidden advantage. If the chosen weapons were swords it was imperative to ensure that both blades were exactly the same length. As sword play could involve much foot work the ground had to be firm and free of any obstructions. In earlier times it had been known for duellists to wear a coat-of-mail under the shirt and seconds were supposed to check the body for that subterfuge.

On occasions metal links were not the only form of defence. In his memoirs Captain Gronow[18] tells of a duel between two French officers in which, after a body check of the right hand side which was normally presented to the opponent, one of the principals changed his shooting position to present his left side to his opponent. Shots were exchanged and he fell. The seconds rushed to him expecting a bloody wound but found that under his waistcoat *several sheets of thick paper were found folded over the region of the heart.* They were strong enough to prevent the ball penetrating but *the blow from the bullet created a sore on the left side which was never effectually cured. The Marquis died shortly afterwards.*

If pistols were the chosen weapons these were subject to close inspection and the flints, powder and balls were supposed to be checked to ensure equality. The pistols were then loaded in the presence of the seconds but there seems to have been no set conditions specifying the size of the powder charge to be loaded into the pistols. Presumably this was a matter of discussion by the seconds but it was an important feature as the charge would have a very obvious effect on the ballistics of the bullet. At these short ranges, the difference in trajectory would probably have been minimal but the velocity of the bullet would be affected and the higher the speed the deeper the possible penetration of the bullet and the greater its expansion if it should it strike bone. However before firing the pistols there was one final safety check to be made. Should the bullet fail to find its human target then it would continue for some distance before falling to earth and therefore might hit an innocent bystander, making it vital to ensure a clear, safe, field of fire behind each shooter.

One obvious decision of major importance was the choice of the distance at which shots were to be exchanged. In the days of the sword this distance was easy to decide by using the length of the sword blade as a marker but pistols presented more of a dilemma. At one time the fashion was that the

---

[18] *Reminiscences and Recollections of Captain Gronow,* 1810-1860, 2 Vols. 1889

more serious the insult the shorter the range. According to the *British Code* ten paces of not less than 30 inches was generally acceptable but the final choice was made by the seconds. With this pacing the distance would be 300 inches, 25 feet or 7.5 metres.

Assuming the pistols were now loaded the opponents would be in their places standing in the normal position of turned sideways so as to offer as small a target as possible. The seconds now handed them the pistols but the author states that the action of the pistol should not be cocked. The author was very particular about how the loaded pistol was to be passed to the shooter. It was to be placed in the shooter's left hand with the barrel pointing in the opposite direction of the opponent and held halfway along the barrel, the duellist then reached across with his right arm and grasped the butt in his right hand. He was than in a position ready to bring the pistol up to his firing position but with the barrel pointing down.

The author does not say so but a command to prepare to shoot must have been given and the final order to fire could be either by voice or by some signal such as dropping a handkerchief. A more elaborate form of signalling is advocated in *The Only Approved guide through all the stages of a quarrel* by Joseph Hamilton published in 1829. He stipulated that a white handkerchief was placed on the ground equal distance from the duellists and one second would pull the handkerchief away by a cord so allowing the opponents to fire.

At this point there were several possible outcomes, the obvious being that each duellist fired at his opponent but there were alternatives. One duellist might choose to fire his pistol in the air rather than at his opponent and this was usually the end of the affair and honour was satisfied. If both shooters missed it was possible, though not obligatory, for a second shot to be fired and in extreme cases even a third but that was reckoned to be the absolute limit, although the trial of England and others mentioned above shows this was not always the case. Wounding of either opponent was sufficient to halt the duel unless the challenger felt that honour was still not satisfied in which case the duel continued.

Whilst duelling in Britain was largely abandoned by the 1840s, in Europe and America it continued to flourish. A pamphlet published in America in 1858 by an ex-Governor of South Carolina, John Lyde Wilson, and entitled *The Code of Honor or Rules for the Government of Principals and Seconds in Duelling* is even more precise in the definition of the duties of the seconds. He states that if the attempt to deliver the written challenge is denied by the recipient the second was to demand in writing an explanation and if that was not forthcoming he too was to issue a challenge. Far more excessive is his idea that each second was to have a loaded pistol and, should either duellist fire before the command had been given, he was at liberty to shoot the offender.

In the pamphlet the author includes an outline of what he claims was an *Irish Code of Honour* agreed in 1777 by representatives from the Irish Counties. It goes into greater detail about the severity of the insult and sundry other details and says that the challenged had the right to choose the weapons and the site of the duel but the challenger decides the distance. The time of the duel and firing regulations were at the combined discretion of the seconds and the weapon of choice had to be a flintlock pistol with a smooth-bored barrel of no more than nine inches. Percussion pistols were permitted but only if both duellists agreed.

The Irish had a reputation of being keen duellers and *The Times* newspaper of the period carried frequent reports of Irish duels. The popular play, *The Rivals*, written by Sheridan in 1775, features one character, Sir Lucius O'Trigger, an irascible Irishmen only too ready to issue challenges. Sheridan in his play *School for Scandal, 1777*, works in a description of a fictional duel and mentions the use of swords and pistols. These references would surely have been well appreciated by the audiences of the period.

Top quality, cased pair, of duelling pistols by Henry Walklate Mortimer c1785-90.

The pistols have octagonal barrels of 28 bore, a middle-sized ball, with sights and full stocks with finely chequered butts. The pistols have set triggers, now more or less a standard fitting found on many pistols of the period. The mahogany case holds the usual accessories including a conventional powder flask and bullet mould. The lid has a trade label and is secured by hooks engaging with studs. This maker was counted as top class and had royal patronage and later held a contract to supply firearms to the Royal Mail coaches. He produced a wide range of firearms and had shops in central London.

Chapter 3:
The Pistols

Locks

The majority of British duels took place during the eighteenth century and early nineteenth century which was the period of the flintlock pistol. Since each duel normally required only one shot to be fired it was obviously essential that the pistol should be reliable and function as perfectly as possible and for this reason the mechanical action of the lock was vital. The flintlock mechanisms of the top quality duelling pistols of the period were as mechanically perfect as possible and represent the acme of the lock-makers' skills.

Lock showing roller bearing on frizzen spring, damp-proof pan, sliding-bolt safety-catch and contoured trigger guard
[Chapel Bay Fort Museum]

The basic spark-generating action of the lock or firing mechanism remained unchanged from the 17th to the 19th century although there were modifications designed to improve its function. The internal components of the mechanism were fitted on the inside of a flat, shaped lockplate often engraved with the maker's name and some decoration. On duelling pistols the decoration was often little more than incised line patterns.

Lock making was a skilled craft and although the name engraved on the plate might be that of the retailer it was no guarantee that he had made the lock. The same situation applied later in the 19th century when some top-class London gunmakers sold guns fitted with ready-made locks purchased from makers in Birmingham. The same situation applied in London in 1760 as is clearly shown by evidence given at the trial of Richard Hewson[19]. He was accused of stealing a number of locks from the premises of Thomas Stamp who described himself as a *gun-lock maker* although the stolen items were listed as being the property of George Vernon, George Haskins and Richard Edge[20], all recorded gunmakers of the period. Stamp explained that two locks were originally the property of Thomas Jourdan and these were identified by the letters TJ which he always stamped on the inside of the lock. Hewson, the alleged thief, tried to sell them and asked three shillings for the pair of pistol locks but the maker reckoned that two shillings and sixpence was their real value.

Stamp stated that he made locks for two of the gunmakers. Haskins, one of the named gunmakers, giving evidence stated clearly *We imploy(sic) Mr. Stamp to get us up locks and then we mark them with our names.* Hewson claimed to have bought the locks from a Richard Melvin and after character witnesses had been called the verdicts were that Melvin was guilty and sentenced to be transported while Hewson was found not guilty.

Whilst the lock plate was fairly simple, to make the tumbler was complex in design and had to be carefully shaped to ensure the smooth action of the

---

[19] t17600521-31

[20] Richard Edge worked at the Tower of London; George Haskins is recorded in 1756, probably worked for the Hudson Bay Company in 1742. See Blackmore

lock. Part of the tumbler had a side lug which projected through a hole in the lock plate and to which was affixed the cock or hammer that held the flint and this also required care in its shaping. Most duelling pistols had a simple S shaped cock which was both strong and decorative. There were other, more elaborate patterns of cock, including a more decorative French style but the basic S form was by far and away the more common. They all had a separate top jaw, moveable by means of a threaded rod, which was adjusted to clamp the flint in the correct position. On Spanish pistols the cock is much sturdier and with a wide jaw, both features necessary as the Iberian flints were generally harder and more liable to breakage.

For best results the flint was wedge-shaped and it was the thin end that struck small, incandescent particles from the steel. Pistol and musket flints varied in quality with some generating sparks long after others failed to do so. Most flints were reckoned to be capable of producing sparks–around thirty times, after which they commonly lost their edge. Black flints were generally believed to be of superior quality. The number of potential strikes was generally of little relevance to the duellist for he might expect no more than a handful of shots in his lifetime. However he needed to be sure that the flint would function on the first firing and best quality flints were supplied with the pistols.

The majority of flints used in Britain were manufactured in the small town of Brandon in Suffolk but there were other centres of production in the same area. The flints were produced by the age-old skill of knapping which involves striking blocks of flint in such a way as to break off thin flakes. These were then worked to form them into the correct shape and size for pistol or musket. Over the centuries flints of various shapes have been used including some of circular form but the most common form, certainly during the 'duelling' period, was rectangular, wedge shaped. The flint held firmly within the jaws of the cock was often cushioned by a thin strip of lead or leather.

The other vital components of the lock were the springs, of which three at least were necessary. The large main spring provided the driving power to make the cock swing forward to drag the toe of the flint down the face of the pan cover or frizzen to strike sparks. These sparks of molten steel ignited the powder in the pan to initiate ignition. Smaller springs were needed to keep the cover closed over the pan and there was also a spring under pressure holding the trigger in place.

Spring-making was a skill largely gained by experience for, when being shaped, the metal had to be heated to just the right temperature if it was to retain its elasticity. The degree of heat was indicated by the colour of the hot metal and the only way to assess the correct temperature was by eye and only experience gave the maker the ability to decide this accurately. The skill of the spring-makers is confirmed by the number of antique pistols and muskets that still have their original springs in full functioning order.

As the cock was gently pulled back the toe of the main spring slid over the surface of the tumbler until it engaged with a notch, or bent, cut into its surface and in this position, known as the half cock, pressing the trigger had no effect and the pistol was safe. Pulling the cock further back rotated the tumbler so allowing the toe of the spring to ride out of the first notch and engage with the second bent, the full cock position. Pressing the trigger now released the cock, driven by the mainspring, to swing forward to generate the essential sparks.

A small quantity of priming powder was put in the pan situated by the touch hole and was retained in place by a pivoted L shaped plate, commonly known as the frizzen. A small spring held this closed to guard the priming powder from wind and rain but as the flint slid down the face of the upright part of the cover it caused the frizzen to tilt forward so lifting that section covering the pan. This allowed the incandescent sparks to fall into the exposed priming powder. There was slight friction between the tip of the frizzen spring and the base section of the frizzen and to reduce this a small wheel or roller was fitted at the end of the spring or the frizzen. The lip of the pan was constructed with an encircling ridge which helped reduce the chances of any moisture seeping through to the powder.

When gunpowder burns it produces some deposit which, if left untouched, generates corrosion and on top quality pistols the inside surface of the pan was lined with gold, a noble metal, which resists corrosion. As the priming powder in the pan flared up the flame passed through a small hole in the side of the barrel known as the touch-hole. This flame ignited the main charge housed in the rear section of the barrel, the breech, which then burnt rapidly to generate the gas that would expel the ball from the muzzle.

This was the common style of lock fitted in the vast majority of duelling pistols although there were one or two other niceties that were possible additions. There was the set or hair trigger which was a small lever system fitted to the trigger which could be set to allow the tiniest pressure to activate the action rather than needing the normal, steady pressure required. This could be an advantage in duelling since it reduced the time taken to generate the sparks and in theory gave the shooter a slight advantage. It was probably more useful in that it reduced any tendency for the pistol to deviate slightly as the trigger was pressed. However it could also be a problem since the slightest touch or knock might fire the shot before the shooter was ready so leaving him in breach of protocol with an empty pistol.

Many pistols were fitted with a safety-catch comprising a narrow bar set into a groove in the lock plate. With the cock set in the half-cock position the bar could be slid forward to engage with a slot cut into the rear of the base of the cock so locking it and making the pistol safe. Another safety device found in some locks was an internal wedge-shaped metal block known as a detente. When the pistol was held with the barrel vertical the detent engaged with the lock and prevented the trigger activating the action. With the pistol in the normal horizontal position the detente was clear of the action allowing the pistol to be fired.

The Stock

When the lock, the end product of the skills of several craftsmen, was complete it had to be fitted into the wooden body or stock of the pistol. The favoured wood was from the walnut tree of which there were several varieties, all noted for their wood's firmness and ability to withstand shock. Walnut was available in several colours ranging from almost total black to patterned, light-brown and it had two qualities which made it popular with gunmakers. It was readily available in quantity from parts of America and Europe and was a fairly easy wood to work with.

The shape of the stock was of prime importance and a good duelling pistol was one which, when held and raised to the firing position, sat comfortably and firmly in the hand without needing any further adjustment. There is no reason not to suppose that 18th and 19th century top gunmakers did not, as some of those of the 20th century did, perhaps shape a butt to a specific shooter's grip. This supposition appears to have been confirmed on pistols made by Wogdon. Careful measuring of the length and curve of the butt of these pistols has shown clearly that there were variations. It seems reasonable to assume almost certainly that they were adjusted to suit the shooter and the only reason for this would be to ensure a good grip.[21]

The basic pistol stock had a gently curving butt the surface of which was often cut with shallow cross-hatching or chequering to give a slightly roughened surface, making for a firmer grip. Towards the end of the 18th century gunmakers developed a saw-handle grip in which the butt had a small, rear-pointing, top section that extended backwards to sit above the web of the thumb. The basic shape of the butt was also changed making it thicker and with a flatter, broader, pommel section and both features were intended to ensure a firmer grip.

The great majority of ordinary pistols of the period had a full stock that extended along the under-side of the barrel almost to the muzzle. From the

---

[21] Information personally supplied by De Witt Bailey and John O'Sullivan

late 18th century duelling pistols tended to be half-stocked where the wood ended part of the way along the barrel.

Apart from its shape the stock required a great deal of work as various items had to be let into the wood. The lock was the main one and required a considerable recess to accommodate the plate and internal mechanism, but its positioning was vital and great care was necessary not to weaken the stock by removing too much wood. The lock was normally held in place by two bolts which passed through the stock to engage with threaded holes on the lock plate. To strengthen the junction of bolts and stock there was usually a narrow metal side-plate set into the stock giving the heads of the bolts a firm location.

In addition to the lock there were other items, known as the furniture, to be fitted into the stock and they included a trigger mechanism which obviously had to be located close to the lock. That part of the stock which seated the barrel had to be shaped to provide a firm base. There were also a couple of short pipes which held the ramrod and these had to be inlet under the barrel section. On the half-stocked pistols these pipes were secured to a metal rib fitted beneath the barrel.

There was also the trigger-guard which in the early days was a simple oval, metal band encircling the trigger, often with some refined decoration and a rear section curving round on the inside of the butt. The trigger guard frequently terminated in a shaped finial often in the shape of an acorn or pineapple. In an effort to improve the grip a small curved extension or spur was fitted on the bottom, towards the rear of the guard. In the aiming position the second finger of the shooting hand could be hooked around this spur so helping to create a firm, steady grip. By the early part of the 19th century the two features, saw-handle butt and spurred trigger-guard, were common on many duelling pistols.

Ramrod pipes and trigger-guard might be of any metal, but brass - either plain or gilded - was most common. These fittings might well be cast by the gunmaker but they were often mass produced and supplied to the gunmaker and in 1826 a trial records 14 pounds of brass furniture as being valued at seven shillings (approximately £17 today). All of these pieces required careful inletting and on top quality pistols it is often almost impossible to feel the junction of wood and metal so well do the parts fit. Some more ostentatious fittings, such as a small escutcheon to be engraved with the owner's arms or initials, might be fitted in the butt.

This is a good quality flintlock also circa 1790 by Henry Nock.

All the usual features of an octagonal barrel, stepped-lock with safety-catch and set mechanism. Butt with chequering and furniture of steel.

The barrel

The barrel was obviously of prime importance and was generally hand-made. Until the later part of the 18th century the barrels on the majority of pistols were tubular in form but there was a gradual change-over to octagonal ones. The majority of barrels were secured to the stock by a lug and pin fitting; on the lower face of the barrel were two projecting lugs with small holes which were let into the stock and a pin was passed through stock and lug. Later the pin was replaced by a narrow plate which was easier to extract than a pin, should it be necessary to remove the barrel.

On some pistols the barrel was secured to the stock by a stronger more elaborate fitting. The breech end of the barrel was made with a solid, upstanding hook and at the rear end of the barrel seating of the stock was an inset metal plate with a central hole. The barrel was slid into the stock and the hook engaged with the plate and a pin and bar fitting, near the end of the stock, held the barrel in place very securely. On many of the barrels there was sometimes a little gold band decoration.

Since barrels were handmade the bore, or internal diameter, varied but it was essential that it was constant along the entire length as any irregularity could affect passage of the bullet and possibly the aim. At the rear end of the barrel was the all-important touch-hole through which the initiating flame passed. As pointed out, burning powder leaves a deposit and corrosion which, left in place, could clog the touch hole and prevent the pistol firing. It was vital to keep the touch-hole clear and on most pistols little more than a piece of wire or thin spike was needed to do this. However on quality pistols in order to reduce the need to clean the touch hole it was bushed with a pierced gold plug. In the late 18th century the production of platinum was simplified and it became more available and from early in the 19th century platinum plugs often replaced gold on the best pistols.

There was some discussion about the boring of the barrel and Rigby, the Irish gunmakers, argued that a slightly angled bore would improve accuracy[22]. This type of barrel appears quite conventional but very accurate measurements of the wall at the muzzle will reveal slight differences in the thickness between the top of the barrel and the bottom indicating a slight slope. What difference this boring made, as far as is known, has never been put to the test. Rigby pistols were not the only ones to use a slightly angled bore and certainly many of Wogdon's pistols use this system. The effect on the accuracy of the shot appears to have been minimal and experimental work carried out has rather confirmed this[23].

The internal diameter of surviving duelling pistol barrels varies considerably and it would be interesting to know whether the differences were deliberate or accidental or if the customer stipulated the size. This measurement may be expressed in two ways; as a bore size or a calibre. The lower the bore size the larger the diameter whilst the calibre may be expressed in inches or millimetres. Duelling pistols are recorded with bores ranging from 10, 18, 22, 32 to as much as 40. In diameter size this is from .78ins (10 bore) through to .45ins (50 bore). The 10 bore bullet is about the size of a musket ball and 50 bore approximates to a bullet from a modern Colt self-loading 1911A1 pistol.

The bore or calibre of the pistol would affect the ballistics of the bullet although it is doubtful if the seconds would have appreciated these niceties. The larger the bullet the larger would be the charge of powder needed to produce the same muzzle velocity as a smaller one although, at the usual short ranges used in duels this was probably of little importance. Where the difference in size of bullet could be important was in the wound it created on striking the duellist. A larger diameter bullet would probably penetrate less deeply but make a bigger wound possibly increasing the chances of infection. A smaller bullet, perhaps with a slightly higher muzzle velocity, might well penetrate deeper but leave a smaller wound and in the circumstances the difference in possible infection was probably negligible. It has been suggested that as many purchasers of duelling pistols were likely to be military officers they might naturally favour the larger bores having seen

---

[22] See Atkinson
[23] Information personally confirmed by De Witt and John O'Sullivan

the effect of bullets in war but this is supposition. Although the accepted protocol was that the pistol should be smooth-bored some duellers were indeed fitted with rifled barrels particularly with very shallow grooves. When duelling had become target shooting then barrels, particularly on the Continent, were fitted with conventional rifling.

The top flat of the barrel was commonly fitted with sights which were often of silver although some purists questioned the wisdom of them fearing there might be reflections to bemuse the shooter. The top flat was also a popular place to engrave the maker's name. When all the furniture was in place the stock was polished and finished off ready to be cased.

The usual barrel length was ten inches (25cms) but there were exceptions and provided both pistols were identical this was probably not seen as a problem although barrel length would have some effect on muzzle velocity. Within limits the longer a barrel the greater the muzzle velocity.

London-made pistol, c1790.

The lock bears the name H. Nock who was a very prolific supplier of military arms as well as supplying the Royal Mail Packet boats. The trigger guard has the early form of extra spur to improve grip. The lock with set trigger has been converted in the 19th century to the percussion system and the plate has been carefully modified to accept the decorated drum fitting. Such conversions were obviously much cheaper than purchasing a new set of duellers.

Cases

Until the later part of the 18th century pistols were apparently sold in cloth bags or plain wooden boxes but from the 1750s and 1760s gunmakers began to supply special wooden cases, the majority fashioned from oak, to house their pistols. Later mahogany became popular although many gunmakers still favoured oak. It was also around this period that the gun makers began to exploit the concept of publicity and adverts and they glued inside the lid of the case either a trade card or a properly produced trade label.

The design of the cases varied in detail but most had some form of security fitting; some with conventional locks and a key whilst others had pivotted hooks on the front of the box which rotated to engage with projecting studs on the lid. There were other features such as brass corner-fittings or carrying-handles, some of which were carefully inset into the lid of the case. Very rarely the wooden case was supplied in a leather outer case but this was unusual.

The inside of the case was usually covered with green baize and divided into sections shaped to hold the various accessories. On British and American cases these divisions were commonly made up by straight fences whilst the Continental cases tended to be more elaborate with contoured sections, each designed for a specific accessory. Many cases had small, triangular, corner sections with fitted lids, often with a small ivory knob, and these were used to hold a selection of balls.

The pair of pistols, positioned butt to muzzle, was usually fitted at the centre of the case. The enclosed accessories followed a general pattern but of course with an expensive purchase such as duelling pistols the client might specify certain items. Almost without exception the case would have a bullet mould. The great majority of these were of the scissors type, comprising two pivoted-arms terminating in sections hollowed out so that, when the arms are closed, the two parts meet to form a cavity of the correct internal diameter. In this section there is a small hole through which the molten lead was poured and after a short time this cooled to form a correctly sized ball. When the arms were opened the ball dropped out but it had a small 'tail' or sprue created at the point where the lead was run into the mould. This had to be removed and the two arms of the mould often had sharpened sections which served as cutters to remove the sprue. The ball would then have to be polished to ensure the surface was as smooth as possible. Smooth bore barrels were commonly loaded directly with the plain ball but when loading a rifled barrel it was usual to ensure a tight fit by wrapping the ball in a small leather or cloth patch. Experts such as Robert Wogdon (see above) apparently wrapped the ball even for smooth bore pistols.

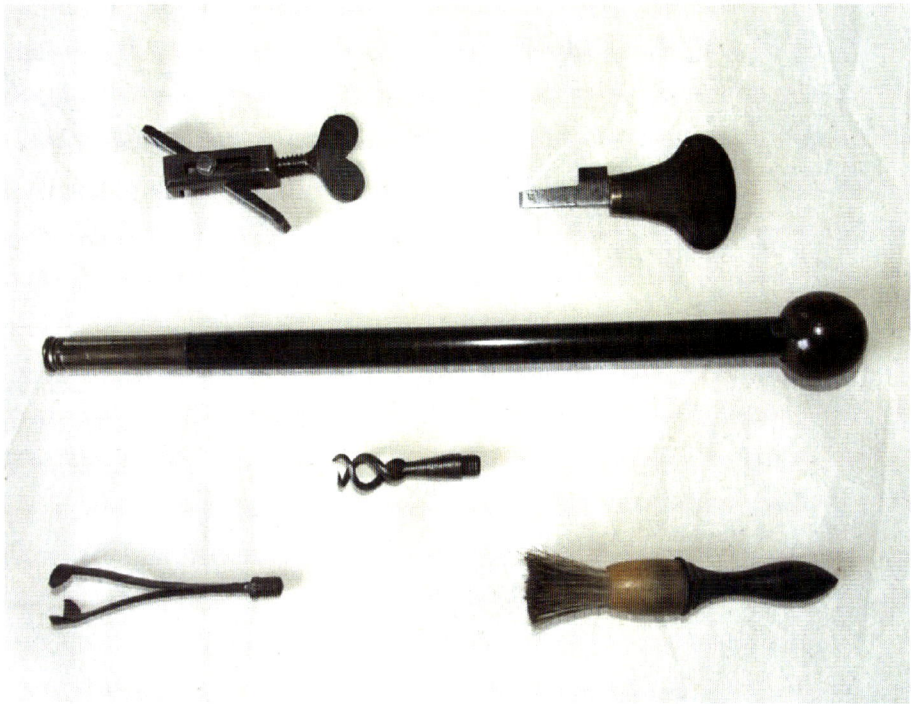

Representative tools

Top left main spring clamp   top right turn screw

Centre ramrod and worm

Bottom ball grip   powder brush

[Chapel Bay Fort Museum]

Equally as important as the bullet mould was the powder flask, commonly sited in a compartment set between the pistols. Two main types of flask were used with the two- or three-way flask being the more common. This had an oval-section metal body, usually leather covered. At one end was the narrow tubular charger, fitted at the base with a spring-operated cut-off. If the finger was placed over the open end of the tube, the cut-off opened and the flask inverted, powder ran out to fill the charger. Releasing the cut-off closed off the charger which now held the correct amount of powder. The body of the flask might have a removable plate at the base which covered a small, internal compartment sufficiently large enough to hold a couple of spare flints. On more elaborate, three-way flasks, at the opposite end, next to the charger another small pivotted plate covered an internal, tubular compartment to hold two or three bullets.

Another commonly used powder flask was much simpler with a plain metal, pear-shaped body with a similar charger. A few of both types had adjustable chargers which could regulate the size of the thrown charges.

The quality of the gunpowder was important and although all types of powder contained the usual components of sulphur, charcoal and saltpetre their proportions and quality could vary. Even more important than the composition was the size of the grains – powders with a small or fine grain tended to burn faster than large grain powders and with some early firearms two types of powder were supplied. A normal, rather coarse grain was for the main charge and a finer grain for the priming, but there seems to be no evidence that this practice was adopted for duelling so it may be assumed that a fine grain powder was used for both main charge and priming. For the dedicated duellist, and there were some, it is quite possible that they checked the quality of the powder using a tester to assess the burning rate and explosive power. These devices varied from very simple forms when a small charge of powder was fired and the blast pushed against a plate, the amount of movement giving some idea of the strength of the powder.

Whilst most pistols had an attached ramrod many cased sets included an extra rod which was also used as a cleaning tool. Should a pistol be loaded but for some reason the shot was not fired then the ball had to be extracted from the breech. For this task there was a worm, rather like a miniature corkscrew, which was fitted to the end of the rod, which was then pushed down the barrel until the worm engaged with the bullet. A few turns ensured that the worm was firmly embedded in the ball and then, hopefully, the bullet could be withdrawn.

Three-way powder flask showing ball section and charger
[Geear Collection, Chapel Fort and Museum.]

The worm could be unscrewed from the end of the rod and replaced by a jag which was a short rod cut with a series of sharp projections. A piece of material was wrapped around it and the ramrod now served as a cleaning rod. A third fitting was sometimes included and that was a small, tubular powder container. Fitted to the end of the rod it was filled with powder and held vertically and the pistol barrel was lowered down over it until it reached the breech. At this point pistol and rod were inverted and the powder was deposited directly into the breech, ensuring that none was lost by adhering to the inside surface of the barrel as it might do if simply poured in at the muzzle.

These were the basic contents of the case but there were some with extra items such as turnscrews or short screwdrivers, including an ingenious type where two with different sized blades fitted together. An essential tool for stripping a lock was a main-spring clamp which could be adjusted to compress and hold the mainspring so permitting it to be lifted clear. Less commonly included were little extras such as small brushes for removing any spilt or loose powder or, very occasionally, a small metal oil container. The physical layout of the components within the case was generally the conventional one with the powder flask at the centre between the pistols but the pattern might well be varied to accept one or two extra pieces such as turnscrews or extra rods.

The advent of percussion

The flintlock system of ignition was simple and efficient but not perfect. Pressing the trigger initiated a series of actions each of which took a small but perceptible period of time: the cock had to swing forward, the frizzen had to tilt, the sparks had to ignite the priming powder, the flame had to pass through the touch hole and finally the main charge had to ignite. Short though each period was the sum total was long enough for the pistol or musket to move and go very slightly off aim and for the shot to be deflected. For a hunter shooting at comparatively long ranges this minute deviation was magnified and could result in a complete miss. For the hunter another drawback of the flintlock was the puff of smoke from the priming which preceded the shot and might startle the quarry. In a duel at short range the effects were probably negligible.

Efforts to overcome this problem were various and complex but thanks to the efforts of a Scottish clergyman, Alexander Forsyth, early in the 19th century a solution using a percussive system was eventually developed. In order to circumvent the patent held by Forsyth there were many attempts to adapt the detonating qualities of chemicals in a variety of ingenious ways such as quills, pellets and paper caps but the copper cap was dominant.

By the 1820s the percussion cap was firmly established and a simple, more positive system of priming was achieved. The cock, flint, pan and frizzen were removed and, instead of a touch hole, there was a small column with a central hole passing through to the breech. Over this column, the nipple, was placed a small, thimble-like copper cap. The cap often had slightly corrugated sides that expanded to give a slight but sufficient grip to keep it in place on the nipple. The inside of the base of the cap was coated with a detonating chemical which, when struck and pressed against the top of the nipple by the flat-nosed hammer which had replaced the cock, exploded with a flash to ignite the main charge. Pistols using the new cap became very popular and it was no surprise that gunmakers soon began manufacturing duelling pistols using the percussion system. At first duelling ethics forbade their use but after a time they were permitted if both principals approved.

When this new system was established the owner of a cased set of flintlock duelling pistols was faced with choices, he might just keep his, now, old-fashioned pistols, or replace them. This meant he could either purchase a new set which would be expensive or else have the flintlock converted to the new system, a much cheaper solution. There were two main conversion systems from flint to percussion, the slightly more positive way was to adapt the lock and fit a new barrel with an integrated nipple.

The other cheaper method was to use a drum conversion. The touch hole was drilled out and in its place was fitted a small pierced drum with a projecting nipple. The other changes were with the lock itself and the pan, frizzen and spring were removed and any holes in the lock plate filled in. The plate needed some slight modification to accommodate the nipple and the cock was replaced by a solid-nose hammer. The position and mechanism of full and half-cock remained unchanged. The gunmakers were obviously only too ready to supply cased sets of percussion duelling pistols and these differed but little in style and contents from earlier examples. One change was in the accessories, for most cases now included a circular tin containing percussion caps either manufactured by one of the main suppliers such as Cooper or Eley or else fitted with the gunmaker's own label. It was not uncommon for an extra rod or turnscrew or oil bottle to be included as well.

Many pistols of the late 18th century were converted to the new system and collectors need to be aware that, in some cases, in order to increase the value, the percussion pistol is re-converted back to the original flintlock. It is sometimes possible to detect the changes by a close examination of the lockplate which may reveal traces of holes being filled in and indicating a change of fittings..

Chapter 4:
Duelling in decline

Duelling had become an accepted part of the culture of Great Britain and was relatively common in the early part of the 19th century with aristocrats, members of parliament and even Cabinet Ministers involved. However a gradual change of attitude gathered momentum and opposition increased and by the 1840s duels were rare. There was no single reason for this decline but rather a gradual feeling by the public, particularly the upper and middle classes, that it was a rather barbaric tradition out of place in a modern society. The rather gaudy, boisterous life-style, common under the Prince Regent had been somewhat modified and softened during the reign of William IV. The accession of Queen Victoria in 1837 with a more feminine life style may well have played some part in the decline and she certainly expressed herself on the matter. Another factor which may have had some bearing on the demise of duelling was the change of British society from a basic, rural one to a more modern one with great mechanical developments. Another possible factor may have been that this was also the period when organised police forces were developing.

Surprisingly part of the growing objection to duelling was that it had spread from what might be called the aristocracy or upper classes and was now indulged in by the middle and trading classes. One particular duel in 1838 involved a linen draper and the nephew of an innkeeper and resulted in the death of one principal. The case was widely reported and condemned by the public. There was a trial with a verdict of the death penalty which was commuted to imprisonment.

In 1840 there was a sordid series of events involving the autocratic Lord Cardington which caught the public eye [24] and even more of the glamour of the duel disappeared. Public opinion became even more organised and specific groups dedicated to the abolition of duelling were formed and the Queen began to take a personal interest and may well have had some influence on the Prime Minister. One big step came in 1844 when Robert Peel's government, in effect, forbade army officers from fighting a duel. It was not so much a formal banning as a threat of what would happen if any officer was involved. The Articles of War which set out details of an officer's conduct now included steps to be taken to reconcile any quarrelsome individuals and in future any officer participating in a duel would be tried by a Court Martial and, if found guilty, cashiered or discharged in disgrace. A further deterrent was that should an officer be killed in a duel his widow would no longer be entitled to an army pension, thus winner or loser in the duel would be in trouble. The new rules did not mean the final and complete rejection of duelling in this country but they certainly curtailed it and by the mid 19th century it may be said that British duelling was over.

The hilt of a Schlager, the sword used in the stylised-style of German Students' duels intended to supply duelling scars with minimum risk.
[Thomas Del Mar]

---

[24] See Hopton and Baldick

Chapter 5
Duelling abroad

Whilst the duel withered in Britain it continued to flourish elsewhere in the world and the Continent saw sword and pistol duels being fought almost to the present. In Germany the ritualistic *mensur* was popular. It was not really a duel but rather sought to give students the chance to acquire duelling scars without the ultimate risk of death. It was rather a test of nerve and participants used special swords known as *Schlage* with straight blades and large, barred hand guards. The opponents stood their ground with much of the body protected in various ways and the object was to strike the opponent's face leaving a scar. The *mensur* was common in German Universities and was actively encouraged during the Third Reich as were genuine duels although this policy was later discarded.

Obviously with the demise of the duel proper the demand for duelling pistols diminished but in its place target shooting became something of a social grace. Cased sets of target pistols were similar to the duelling ones and the contents, especially from the Continent, were mostly highly decorated. The pistol barrels were often fluted, the butt was of conical form, curved, frequently fluted and widened towards the base. The pistols were commonly rifled as accuracy was an integral objective of target shooting but this meant that the bullets were tight fitting in the barrel. Ramming the ball down into the breech was difficult and sometimes required the use of a mallet to drive the bullet home. Continental cases usually contained more accessories than the earlier duelling pistols. Another common feature of Continental cased sets is the method of dividing the internal space. The British and US gunmakers tended to use simple straight fences but the Continentals used contoured fences specially shaped for the item.

There was a brief fashion for 'mock duelling' when the principals donned protective clothing and shot at one another using special wax bullets but this seems not to have caught on in Great Britain.

By the mid-19th century, encouraged by the patriotic Volunteer movement, pistol shooting and from the 1850s, revolver shooting grew in popularity. In the mid 20th century, as mentioned above, there was even a simulated duel style when traditional procedures were followed but wooden and paper targets replaced one's opponent. After a couple of shooting tragedies handgun target shooting was virtually outlawed from 1997 and today non-competitive shooting is permitted only on a very limited and legally confined basis. This brought to an end a sport which, for centuries, had enabled both sexes of all ages and condition to compete on an equal basis.

Chapter 6
The Gunmakers

There have been gunmakers in London since the 14th century but they were mostly based in small workshops manufacturing the components of a gun such as locks, brass furniture, springs and barrels. Most were members of the various specialist livery companies of the City of London especially the Armourers and Blacksmiths. Late in the 16th century there were moves to establish one organisation covering the differing companies and in 1605 the gunmakers received letters patent which united them into one body which was recognised by the Board of Ordnance the official purchaser of arms. In 1631 letters patent were granted to the Armourers and Blacksmiths and some associated crafts and finally in 1638 the Gunmakers Company was established.

Most of the workshops were near the Tower of London in the area known as the Minories. Naturally the greater part of their business was with the Board of Ordnance supplying muskets and military pistols but there was a demand for hunting weapons and as demand grew more makers began exploring the civilian market.

From the 1780s to the 1840s the main suppliers of top quality duelling pistols were to be found in London. Before long a number of gunmakers established themselves as the prime suppliers. They also set up shops in fashionable areas of London and sought Royal patronage which was a great help in acquiring a reputation. Their cased sets of duellers were highly priced and praised and status-conscious men made sure that their cases carried the trade labels of the top gunsmiths. In fact it is clear that although the pistols might be engraved with the name of a famous maker it did not mean that all the pistol was entirely their product. It has been well established that Birmingham, in particular, was a supplier of ready-made items which were embellished with the name of London makers.

Although London was seen as the centre of quality production this did not mean that provincial makers were second-rate and many of their products could well match London-made guns. The provincial makers were sometimes behind the times and some of their weapons feature details that were seen as rather out of fashion compared with London pieces. The top London makers with their rich and powerful customers were often able to indulge in the making of beautifully decorated pieces beyond the ability of most provincial makers.

Joseph Manton was probably the most highly esteemed manufacturer but his various sons were equally prized and it was a similar setup with the Egg family beginning with the father Durs. Makers of such status frequently numbered their products and in some cases, the Mantons in particular, surviving records permit numbered items to be dated precisely. Robert Wogdon was seen as the prime maker and was even honoured by having a poem written about him in which he is described as *the patron of leaden death*. Duelling pistols rank high in the collecting field and command very high prices especially if they have a good provenance.

A Selection of Makers

This brief list records the names and relevant dates of some of the better known London gunmakers whose names may be found on examples of the "duelling" period. The list records family names but in many cases there were sons or relatives who traded separately and for full details Blackmore's book has no equal. Published first in 1986 it is still the standard reference and although some extra details and minor corrections have emerged since then, collectors and students will always be indebted to the author.

Provincial makers have been less well researched but are recorded and details of new publications are given in the bibliography.

Archer	1753-1807
Beckwith	1818-1868
Blissett	1822-1864
Bond	1730-1853
Brown	1780-1841
Egg	1772-1835
Forsyth	1807-1819
Harding	1810 -1816
Henshaw	1763-1822
Jover	1775-1810
Mills	1797-1843
Mortimer	1753-1860
Nock	1770-1853
Parker	1793-1841
Parker Field	1842-1852
Purdey	1798-1857
Staudenmayer	1799-1834
Tatham	1770-1835
Twig	1732-1790
Wogdon	1748-1813

Bibliography

Anon (1824) *British Code of Duelling*

Anon (1836) *The art of duelling*

Atkinson, J. (1964) *Duelling Pistols*, London

Baldick, R. (1965) *The Duel* London

Blackmore, Howard L. (1986) *A Dictionary of London Gunmakers* 1350-1850, London

Brown, Nigel (2004-2009) *British Gunmakers*, Vol.1 (2004) London, Vol. 2 (2005) Birmingham, Scotland the Regions, Vol.3 (2009) Index and additional details, Shrewsbury

Douglas, W. (1887) *Duelling days in the army*,

Hamilton, J. (1829 rp 2007) *Duelling Handbook*, London

Hopton, Richard (2007) *Pistols at Dawn*, London

Kiernan, V. (1988) *The Duel in European History* Oxford

Landale, J. (2005) *Duels*

Neal, W Keith & Back, D (1967 & 1978) *The Mantons: Gunmakers* and *The Manton Supplement.*

Neal, W Keith and Back, D (1980) *British Gunmakers-Their Trade Cards, Cases and Equipment*

Noble, Duncan (2009) *The Rapier: history and use of a fearsome weapon*, Ken Trotman Publishing, Godmanchester 2009

Steinmetz A. (1958) *Romance of duelling in all times and countries*, 2 vols

Wilson, J. (1858) *Code of Honor*

Examples of Duelling Pistols

Figure 1:
An officer's duelling pistol made by
Jover of London circa 1775

Typical of the period. It has a full walnut stock with butt cap
and a stepped, signed lock. The maker produced quality
weapons but was not counted among the very top makers.

Figure 2:
A pair of early style duellers by William Brander,
dating from about 1780.

This maker was based in the area near the Tower of London known as the Minories and supplied weapons to the Honourable East India Company. The 10 bore barrels are slightly longer than usual and of one of the larger sizes for such pistols. The barrels are fitted with rear sights and there are indications that there were, at one time, front ones although they are now missing.

Figure 3:
Another later pair by Jover circa 1805-1810

They have walnut half-stocks with the earlier style chequered
butts and later style spurred trigger guards of steel although
the other furniture, including butt escutcheons, is of silver. The
silver caps on the half stocks have some engraved decoration.
The barrels are signed and the locks, which are fitted with detents
and sliding-bolt safety catches, have some gold decoration.

Figure 4:
This pair has locks and barrels signed by the doyen of duelling pistol makers, Robert Wogdon.

They were made around 1785 but in the 1820s were converted to the percussion system using the simple drum and nipple fitting. The locks have sliding safety-catches and are fitted with set triggers to ensure smooth action. The butts have the earlier fashion slightly bulbous butt caps with long side-spurs.

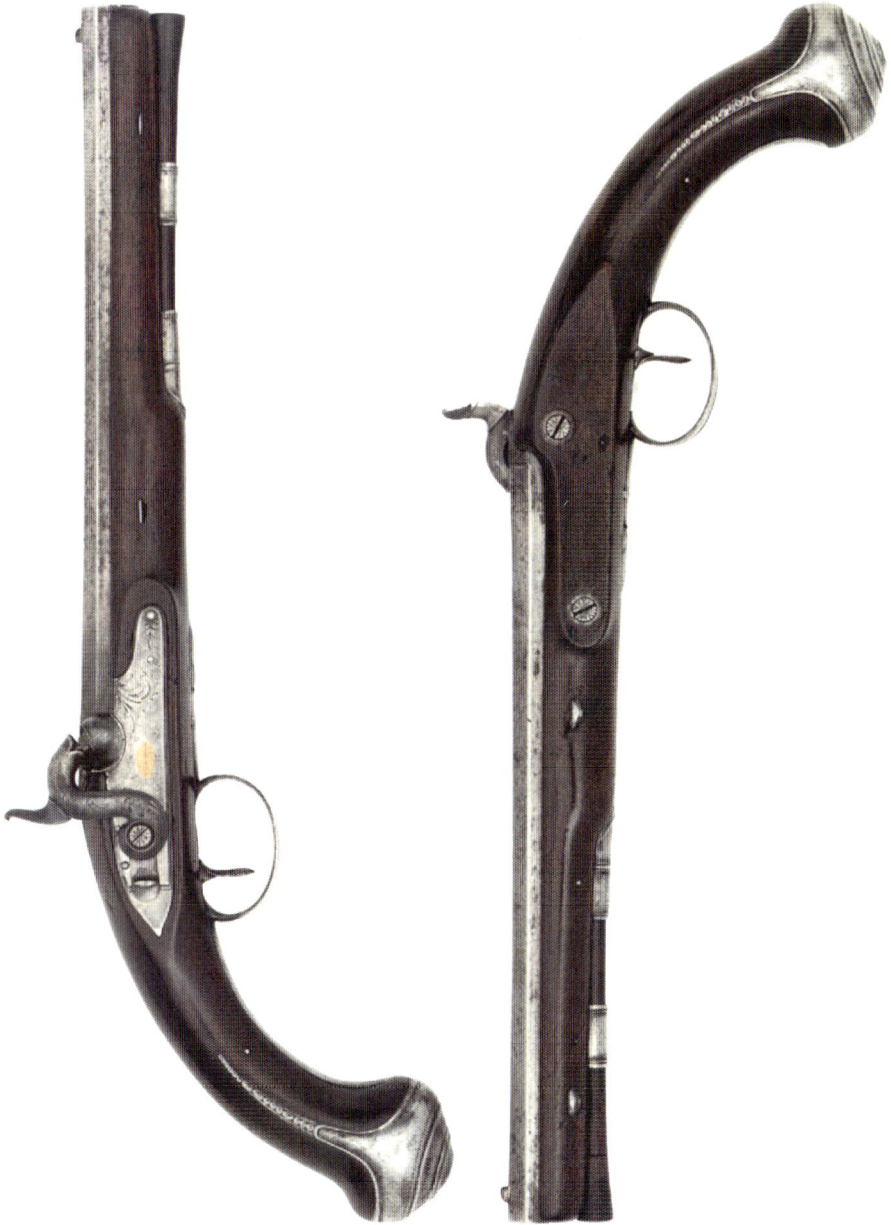

Figure 5:
Another pistol by Wogdon and slightly later in date, c 1790.

Typical of the elegant dueller of the period, fully stocked with an octagonal, sighted 28 bore barrel which is around the average size for such pistols. The stepped lock has the usual sliding safety-catch.

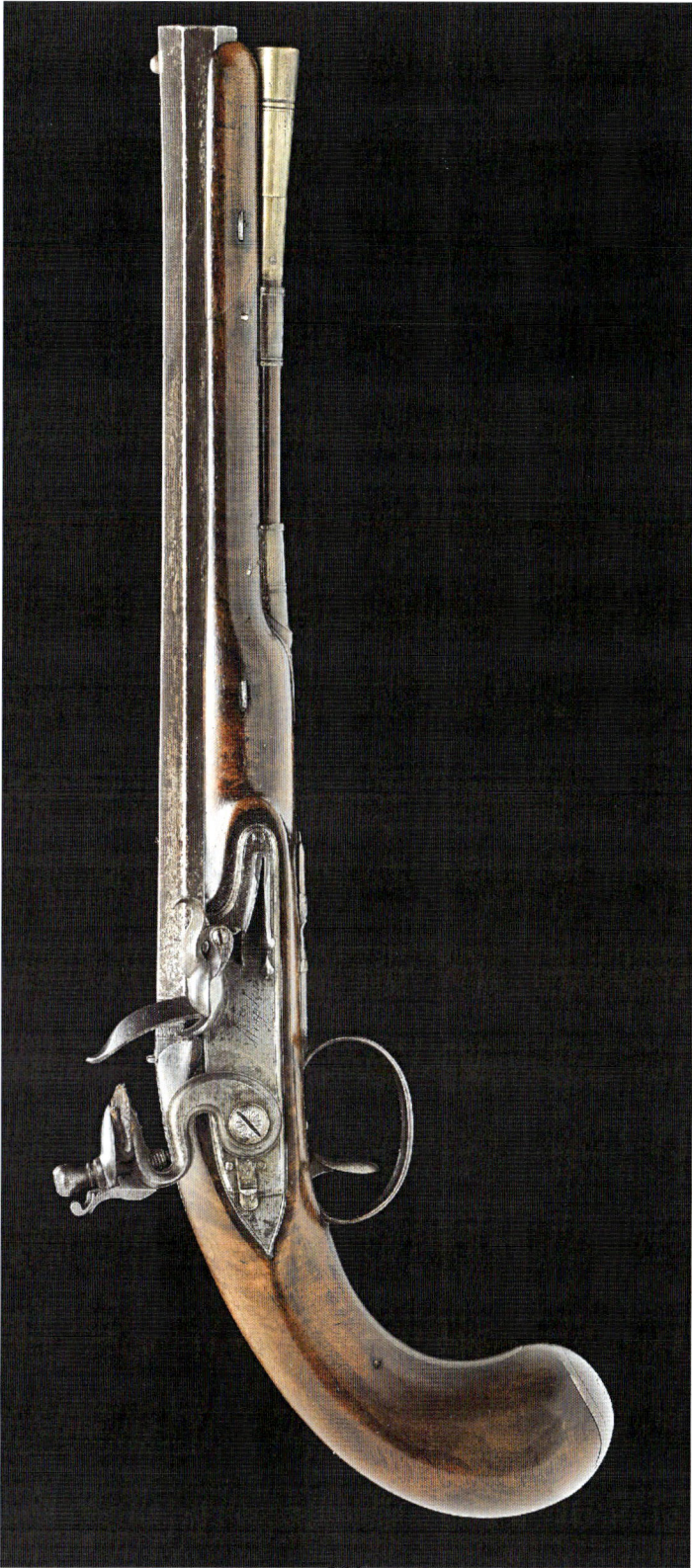

Figure 6:
Another cased pair of similar date but by a lesser
London maker Matthew Limbery.

The full, walnut stocks are typical but the flat-sided butts have, at a later date, been finely chequered, presumably in an attempt to offer a slightly firmer grip for the shooter. It is fitted with a set trigger and there is some simple gold decoration.

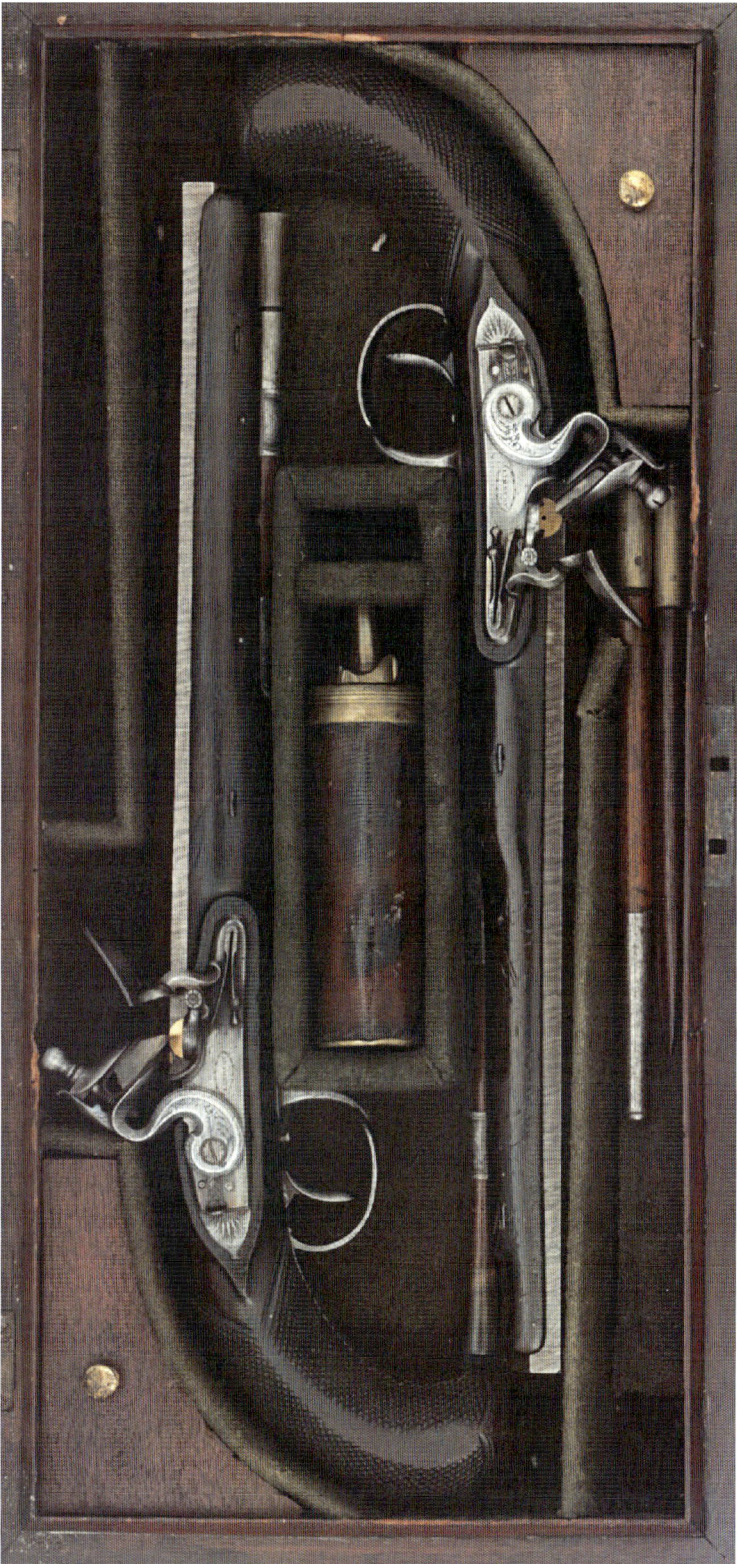

Figure 7:
Made in Dublin by Powell circa 1790, this pair is very similar to the London-made weapons indicating a common style.

The octagonal, sighted barrels are signed and the lock exhibits a new feature, a small roller bearing on the frizzen intended to reduce friction and ensure quick movement. Quality is good with gold vents and the silver furniture includes butt escutcheons engraved with an owner's initials FD. At some time one of the locks was presumably lost or damaged and was replaced with a very similar one, signed Fowler.

Figure 8:
Another example of Wogdon's pistols circa 1790.

The style is elegant with full walnut stocks and steel furniture
and the locks with conventional sliding-bolt safety-catches
and set triggers. The barrels are of 24 bore.

Figure 9:
**A good quality pair of duellers by William Parker of Holborn,
London dating from around 1800 and numbered 2524.**

They have all the typical features of octagonal, sighted barrels
mounted on full stocks with chequered butts. The locks are
signed and fitted with rollers on the frizzen springs but no set-
triggers and unusually are fitted with French style cocks.
This maker manufactured a wide range of products from
truncheons to top class sporting guns as well as equipping
many early police forces.

Figure 10:
Another pair by Jover circa 1800.[25]

In many ways similar to those by Parker with 18 bore barrels
engraved London but bearing Birmingham proof marks; another
indication of the internal trading between suppliers. The pistols
have some common features such as set triggers and roller
bearing but are still basically of the earlier style.

---

[25] See pp 54 & 58 for other examples

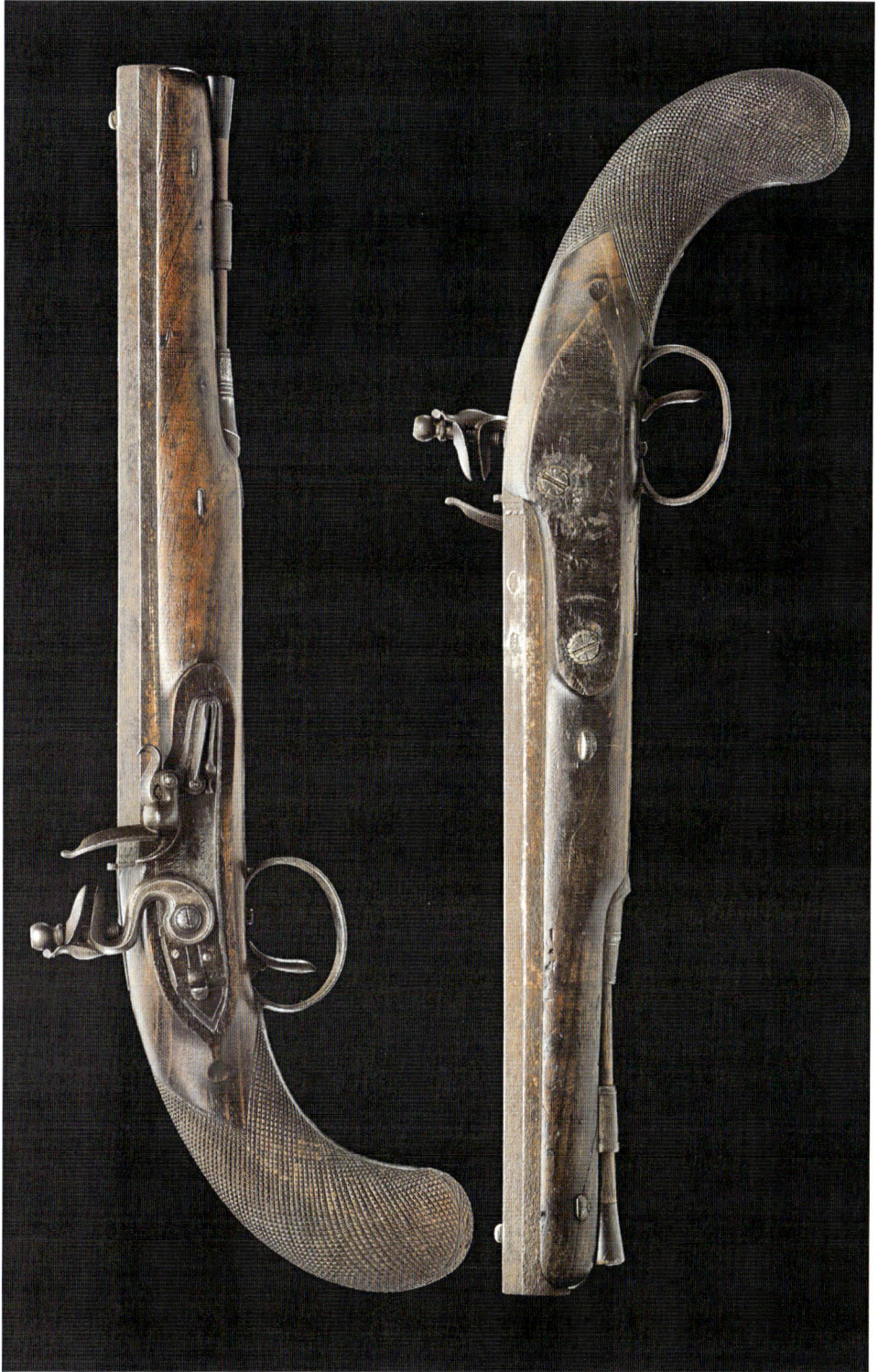

Figure 11:
Pistol by a provincial maker, William Paris of
Derby circa 1800.

Although similar to most pistols of the period it differs in having
some simple, scrolled decoration on the stock and butt which may
be a later addition. The trigger guard is terminated with an urn shaped
finial instead of the more common pineapple. The barrels are
22 bore, about average for such pistols.

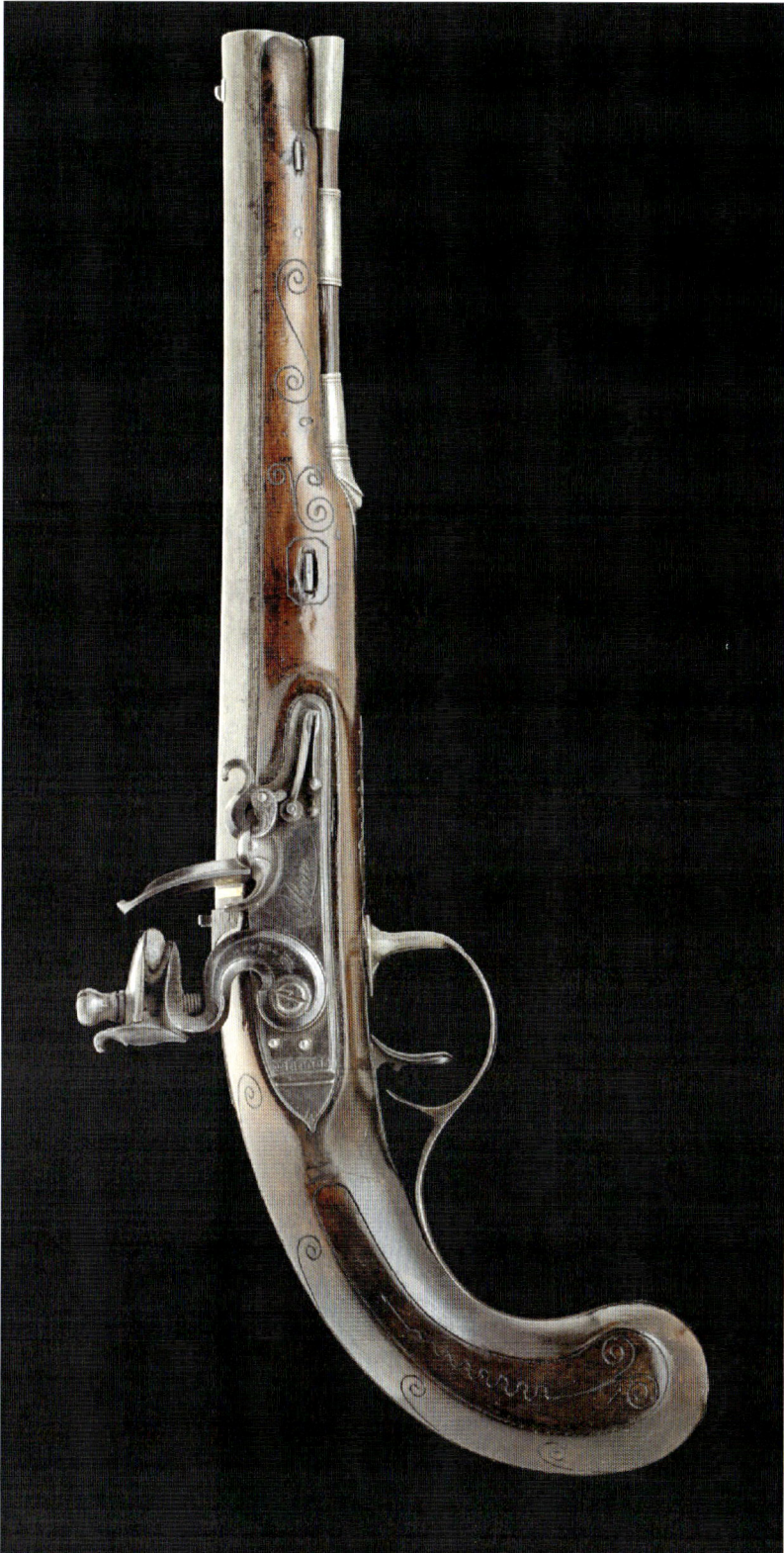

Figure 12:
Another provincial pistol by John Gardner of
Newcastle-Upon-Tyne and dating from 1800.

It was converted to percussion in the usual way by drum and nipple which necessitated a minor modification to the lock plate to accommodate the drum. The barrel is stamped with London proof marks.

Figure 13:
Dating from c 1800 this Irish pistol is by Barrett.

It has an unusually long barrel and is stamped with C 2405. This is a census mark introduced in 1842 when all Irish weapons were supposed to be officially recorded; the letter indicates that this one was registered in Cork. It is fully stocked with the butt chequered and, unusually, fitted with a butt cap.

Figure 14:
A cased pair supplied by the London maker Samuel Brunn
from his shop in Charing Cross and dating 1800-1804.

The pistols are fairly conventional; fully stocked with stepped locks with sliding safety-bolts and escutcheons engraved with initial GT. The case is of oak (many were of mahogany) and the lid has a brass, carrying fitting engraved with the owner's name, Captain G. Taylor who later served as a Lieutenant Colonel in the Canadian Militia.

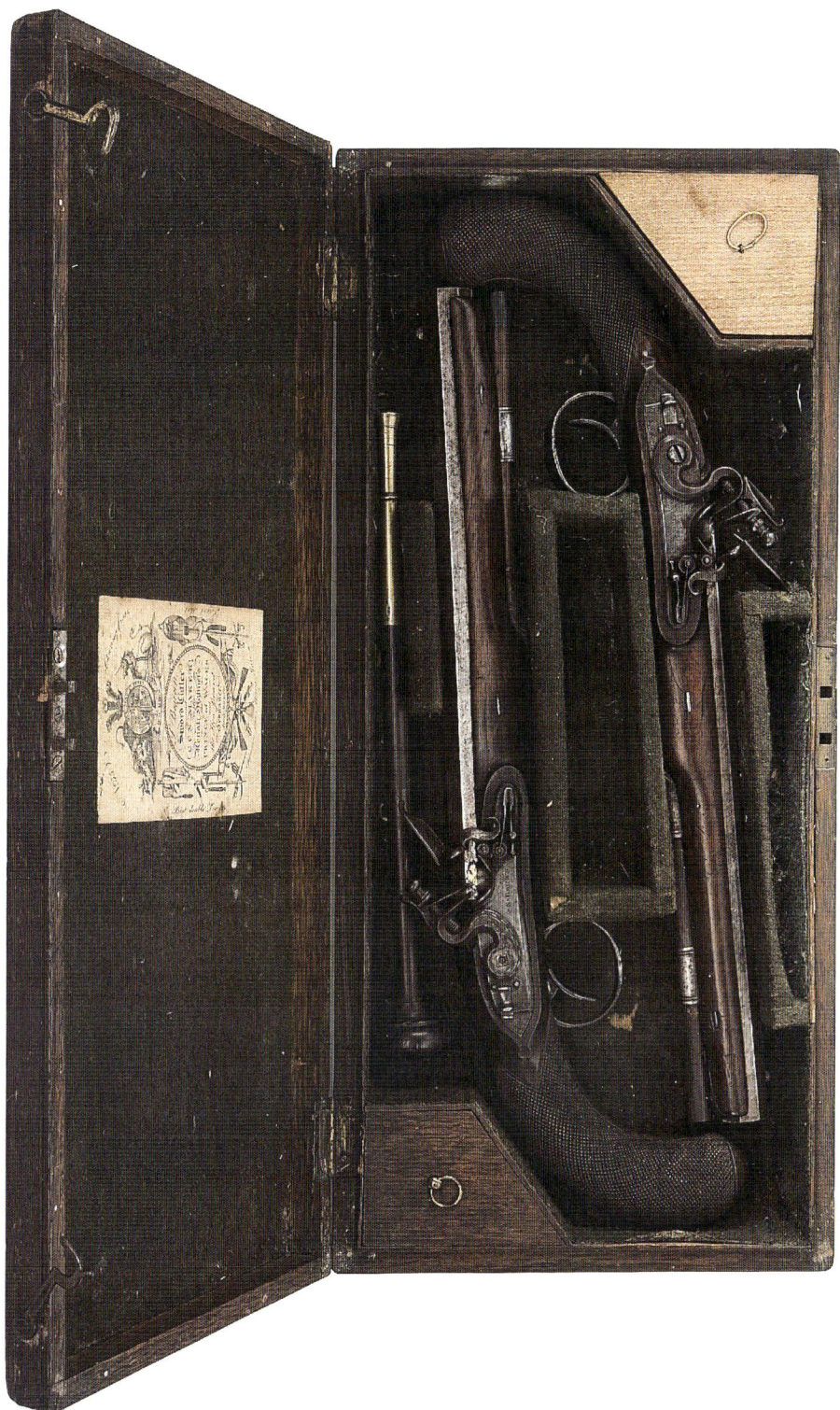

Figure 15:
**Featuring the changes in style this pistol dates from 1806-1810
and was made by a good London maker, H. W. Mortimer
and Son. It is numbered 1357.**

The butt is saw-handled with a top, rear extension and the trigger guard is fitted with the spur extension and the barrel has a platinum plug vent, a feature which begins to appear about this period. The signed lock has all the best features with a detente, rain-proof pan and roller bearing. The half-stock is with engraved steel mounts and the base of the butt has an inset plaque.

Figure 16:
A pistol by one of, if not the best, makers in London,
Joseph Manton, dating from circa 1810
and numbered 5107.

The 40 bore barrel is unusual in that it has shallow rifling, not usually found in duelling pistols; it also has a silver foresight and a platinum plug. The half-stock has a conventional, finely chequered butt with an escutcheon engraved with the letter M and a baron's coronet and has a spurred trigger guard. The extremely fine lock is fitted with a detente and is stamped JB, the initials of Joseph Brazier a maker of quality locks working in Wolverhampton.

Figure 17:
This provincial example dates from circa1810 and was made by a Birmingham maker, Samuel Galton.

Its general style is rather old-fashioned, a common feature of provincial weapons. The stock is fitted with steel furniture and the lock, signed and dated, has the usual sliding-bolt safety catch. The horn tipped ramrod is fitted with a worm.

Figure 18:
Another Irish made pistol this time by
Pattison of Dublin around 1810.

The butt is of the new, saw-handle style but the trigger guard lacks the spur. In common with many other pistols it has the drum and conversion fitting. Like most Irish pistols of the period it is stamped with a census number DC 6314. The lock has a sliding-bolt safety and has some engraved decoration.

Figure 19:
This Irish example also about 1810 by Anglin is
of similar date but retains more of the older style
features such as a full stock.

The lock lacks a safety-catch but is engraved as is the
trigger guard. The census mark is WX 4690.

Figure 20:
**Dating from 1810 this example is by a London
maker Fisher.**

It exhibits a mixture of old and new features with a half-stock,
chequered butt, lock with roller-bearing and fitted with a
detente. The furniture is of steel with a small butt cap and
a trigger guard with typical pineapple finial. The cock is
a replacement.

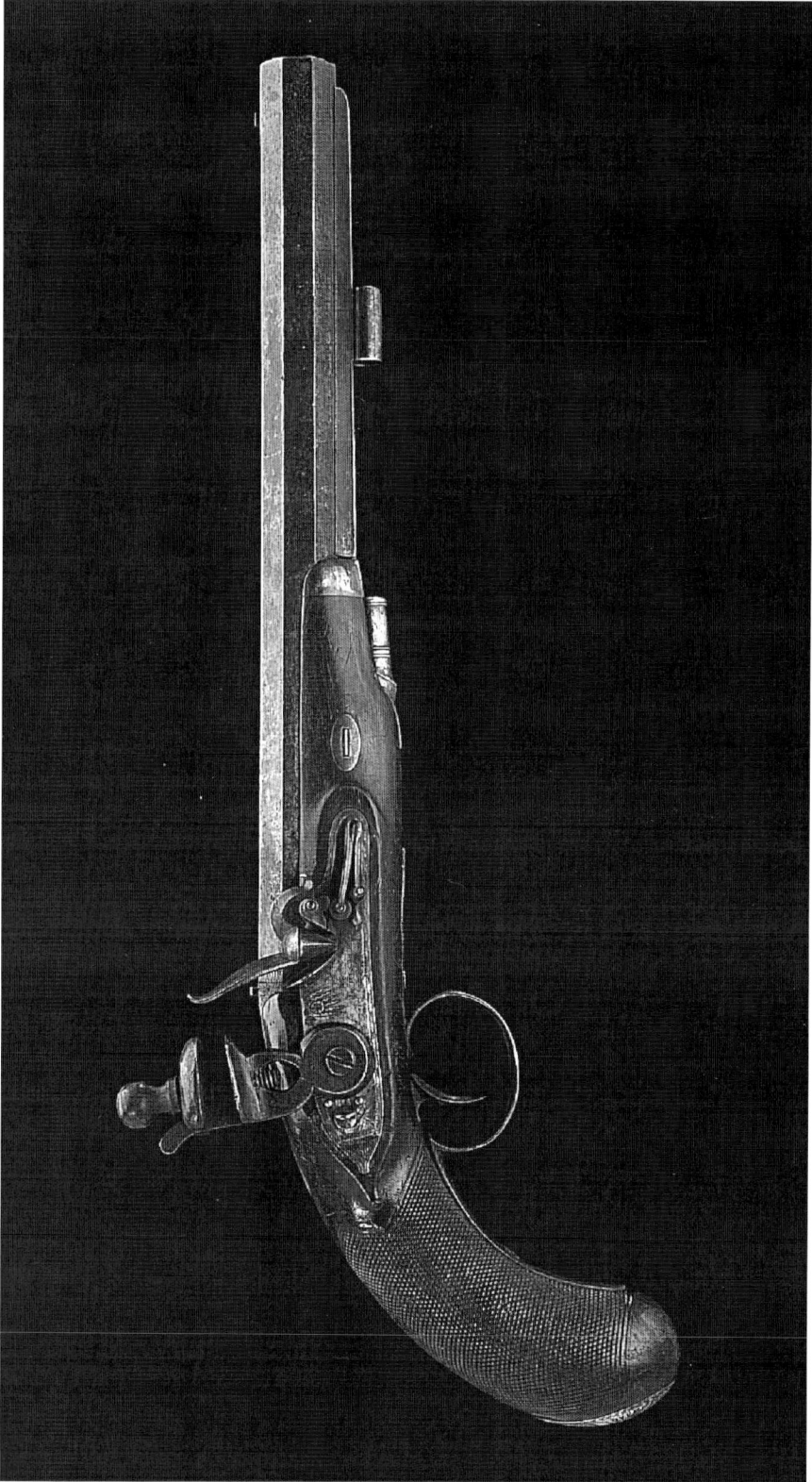

Figure 21:
A cased pair by top London maker Joseph Manton which were probably owned by General Sir Marin Hunter who saw action in the American War of Independence and in India.

The pistols are numbered 6228 and surviving records make it possible to fix an exact dating of 1814. The original case lacks all accessories but has a trade label on the inside of the lid. The pistols are typical of the period with engraved steel mounts and sliding bolt safety-catches. Manton held several firearms patents and the locks are fitted with patented steels numbered 6099 and 6100.

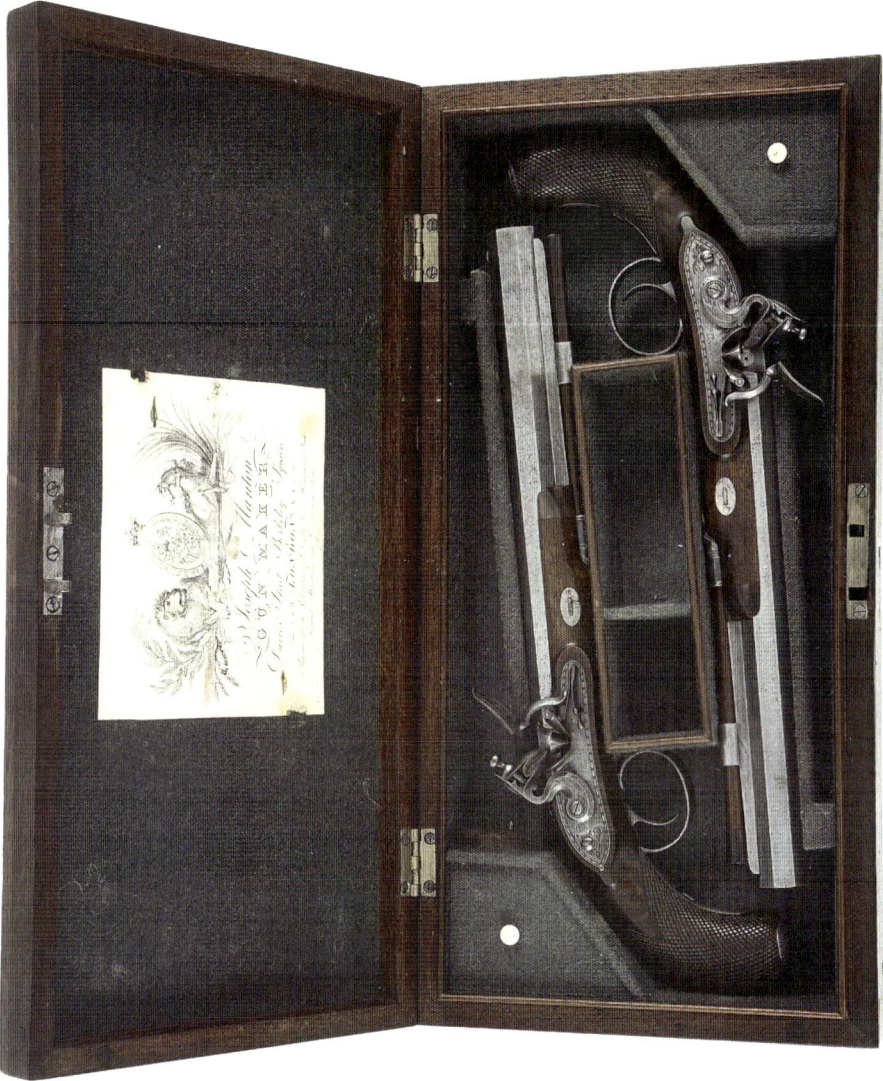

Figure 22:
This elaborately decorated pistol made by W. Ketand & Co
circa 1815 was intended for export to the east.

The octagonal 32 bore barrel has decorative silver inlay and
front sight whilst the full stock is covered with scrolling, floral,
silver inlay. The lock has a decorative plate, damp-proof pan,
roller bearing and the trigger guard has the now common spur.
The cock is far more decorative than normal and is similar
to the French style. Many London makers produced similar
decorative pieces for what must have been a lucrative market.

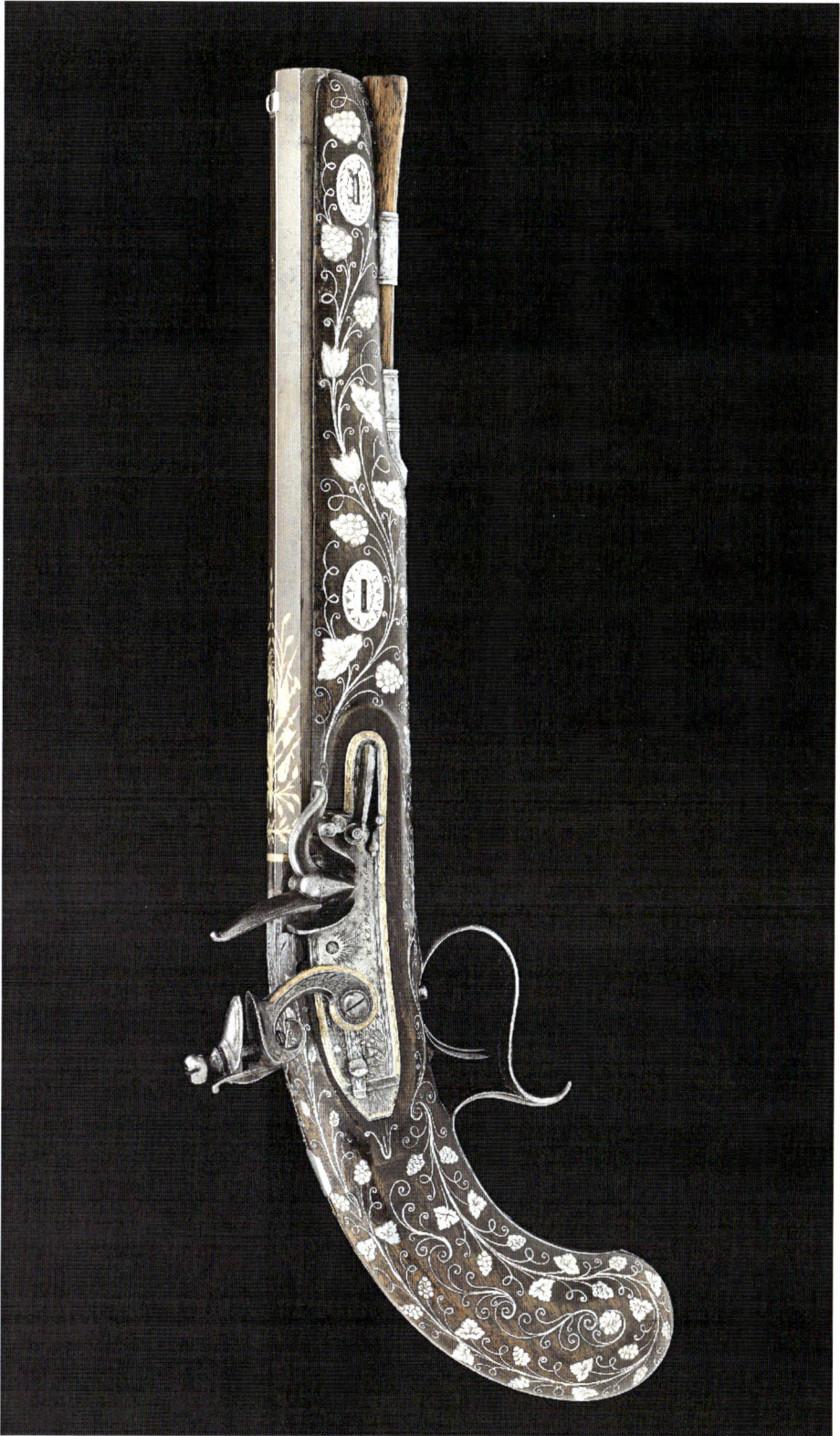

Figure 23:
Another, more complete, cased pair by Joseph Manton
dating from 1815 and numbered 6548.

The 40 bore barrels have some decorative inlay of the now popular platinum but the general style is of the earlier pattern with half stocks, chequered butts, safety catches and simple trigger guard. The locks have patent steels numbered 488 and 489. The brass-mounted, mahogany case has the usual accessories including a bullet mould and a three-way, leather-covered powder flask. The lid has an inset brass carrying handle.

Figure 24:
Another very similar cased pair by Joseph Manton
numbered 6862 and dated to 1816.

The barrels are 40 bore and the steels are numbered 7625 and 7626 and the breeches are stamped Manton Patent but the General style is conventional. The mahogany case holds usual Accessions including a three-way powder flask.

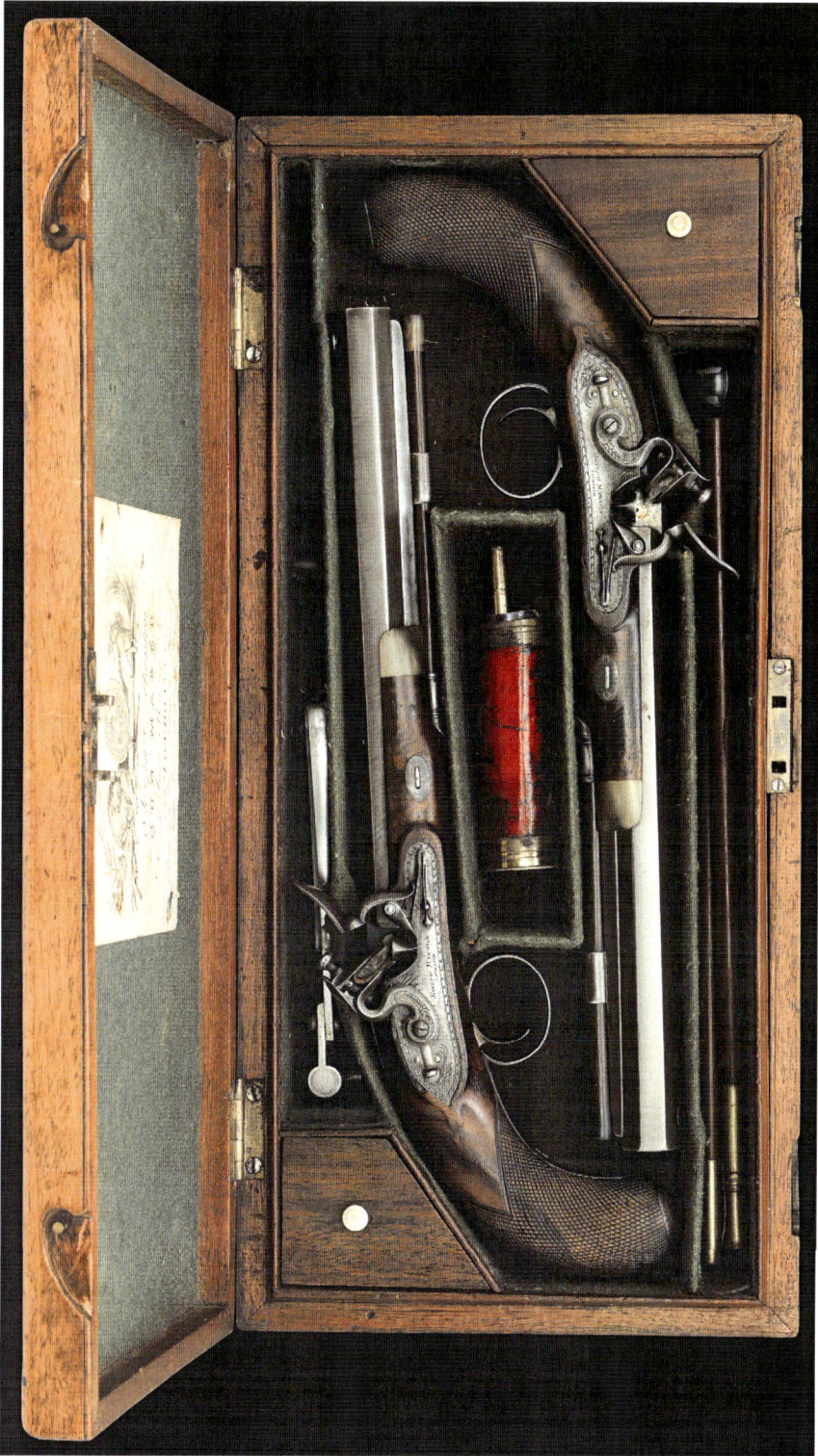

Figure 25:
Percussion pistol by Thomas Manton of Long Acre,
London and dated to 1817-1825.

This maker is later recorded as working in Grantham. The pistol was made as a percussion weapon with an integral nipple with a platinum plug but is otherwise of conventional form. It is half-stocked with chequered butt and simple trigger guard.

Figure 26:
Another provincial flintlock pistol by
Gardner of Newcastle circa 1820.

It is basically of standard pattern but the lock is fitted
with a set trigger mechanism (the adjusting screw is situated
just in front of the trigger). The usual drum and nipple
conversion has been used.

Figure 27:
A cased set by John Manton of Dover Street London rated almost as good a maker as Joseph and made about 1822.

The pistols are numbered 1929 and the 40 bore barrels are rifled, an uncommon feature which might indicate they were intended for target practice rather than duelling. They are also slightly unusual in that they have furniture of blued steel. The well equipped case holds all the normal items plus a small oil bottle and the lid is fitted with a folding carrying handle and carries a trade label.

Figure 28:
A cased percussion pair circa 1830 by H. W. Mortimer
of London but with Birmingham proof marks.

The twist barrels are browned with gold lines at the
breech and with platinum plugs. The trigger guards are
of blued steel and have the commonly used pineapple finials.
They are of conventional half-stocked style and are in the
original oak case with some accessories including a cleaning rod.

Figure 29:
Single flintlock pistol of good quality, dating from around 1830 when flintlocks were going out of fashion. It is by the Holborn gunmaker William Parker.

As pointed out above (p 70) this maker, succeeded by his son-in-law Field, produced firearms ranging from trade guns to top quality sporting guns and duellers. This example has many quality features such as the spurred trigger guard, roller bearing and set-trigger.

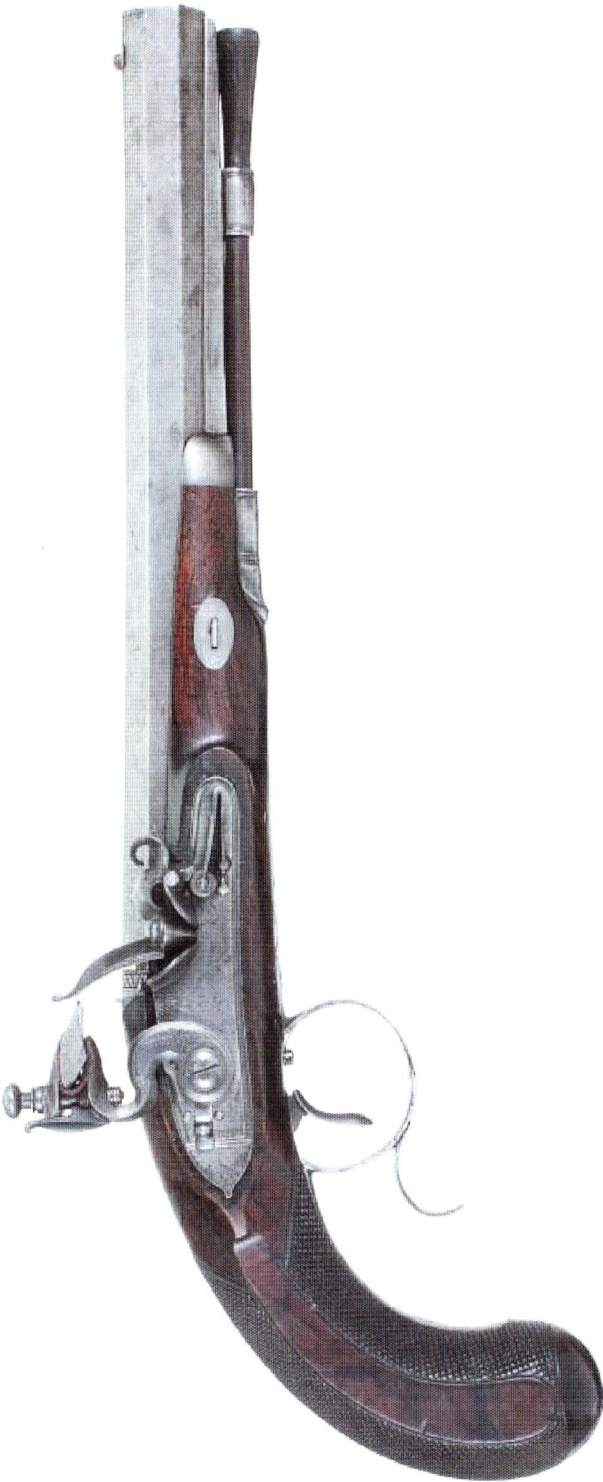

Figure 30:
A French percussion, duelling pistol by Baucheron
Permit à Paris circa 1840.

This is a typical example indicating the differences in design of the general Continental taste with more decoration than that found on British pistols. It is half-stocked with heavy, sighted octagonal barrel and curved chequered butt with expanded pommel. The trigger has a set mechanism and is very slim and straight; the guard with usual spur.

Figure 31:
A most unusual pair of percussion pistols by Samuel Nock[26]
circa 1833 and numbered 7335.

This pair has so many unusual features it seems likely that they were a special customer order. The half-stocks have a flattened, angular form and it has been suggested that the pistols were ordered by someone influenced by the shape of the old Scottish flintlock butts. The locks are of back-action style which is unusual and are signed Samuel Nock Inventit but have conventional sliding-bolt safety-catches. The original case retains some accessories including a fine three-way powder flask.

---

[26] Nephew of the well known Henry Nock.

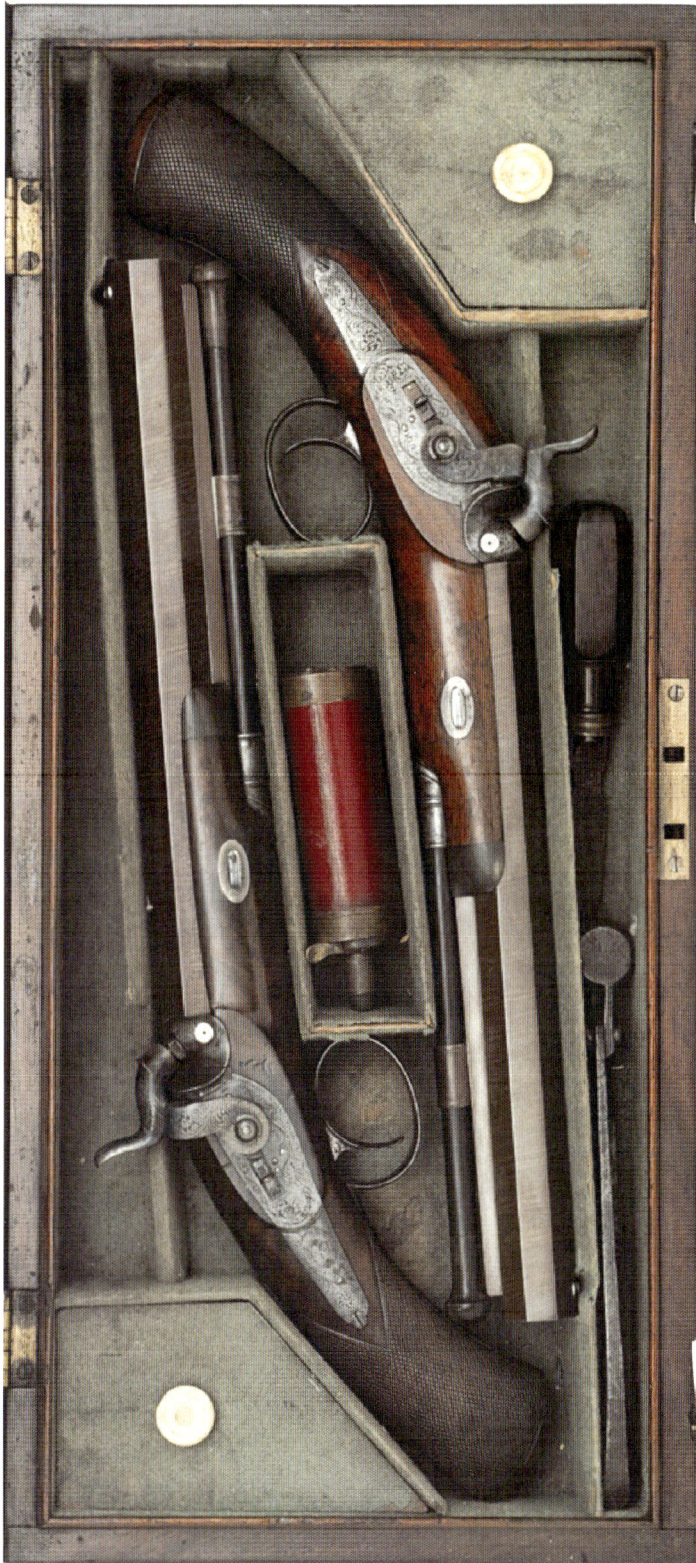

Figure 32:
Cased Irish pair by famous gunmakers William & John Rigby;
numbered 1718 & 1719 and made about 1835.

Sighted octagonal barrels with some platinum decoration and plugs and half stocks which are not of the usual walnut but are of blackened elm with saw-handle butts, spurred trigger guards and fitted with back action locks. The mahogany case has the accessories fitted in a slightly unusual style. The company records state that these were made for a Captain Croft.

Figure 33:
Continental taste was for far more decoration of cases and contents as with this pair by A.V. Lebada of Prague, Austrian Empire (now in the Czech Republic) around 1840.

The octagonal, sighted-barrels blued, signed in gold and numbered 1 and 2. The walnut half stocks have panels of chequering on the butts as well as some carved decoration and silver furniture. The fitted case is of veneered rosewood with a leather lining stamped with decorative gilt foliate patterns. Note the inclusion of a small mallet necessary when loading very tight fitting balls.

Figure 34:
A good example made by a London gun maker,
Lyell, about 1840.

The signed, heavy barrel carries Birmingham proof marks and
the half-stock has blued steel furniture including a trigger
guard with popular pineapple finial. The lock has a safety catch
and a set-trigger fitting. The whole pistol is of good quality despite
the fact that the maker was not counted among the best.

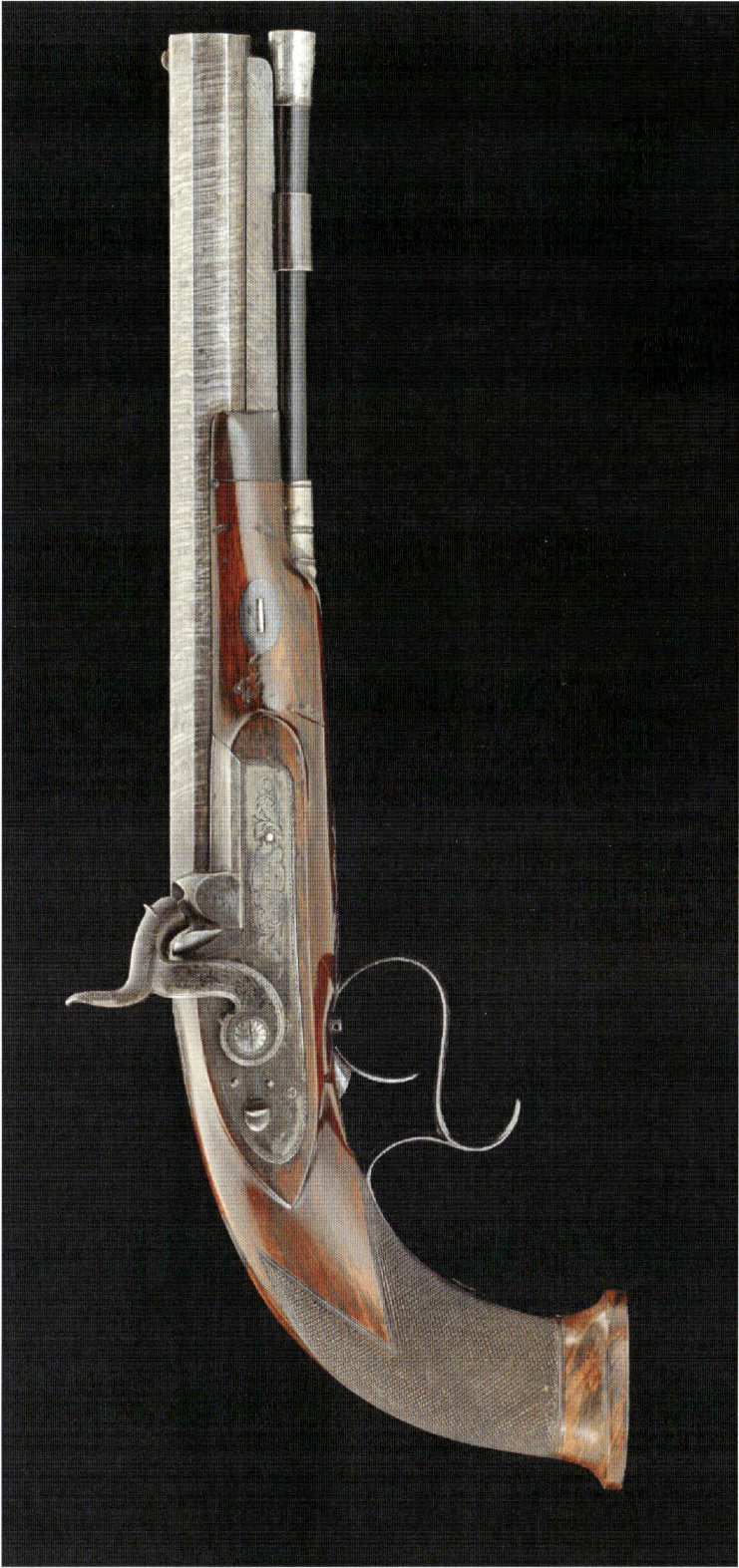

Figure 35:
A top-quality pair by Westley Richards, a Birmingham maker with a retail shop in New Bond Street London; they date from around 1840.

The sighted 28 bore barrels have some decoration and the locks are fitted with détentes and sliding bolt safety-catches. The walnut stocks have Continental style pommels and the pistols are in the original mahogany case with a whole range of accessorises including a small ivory box to hold the percussion caps.

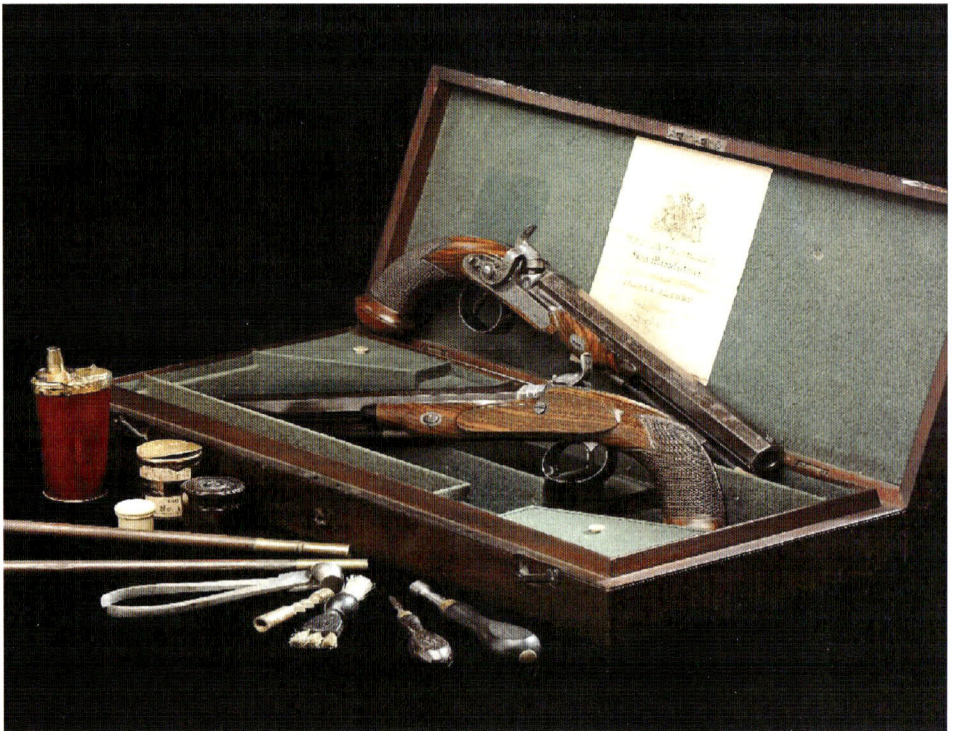

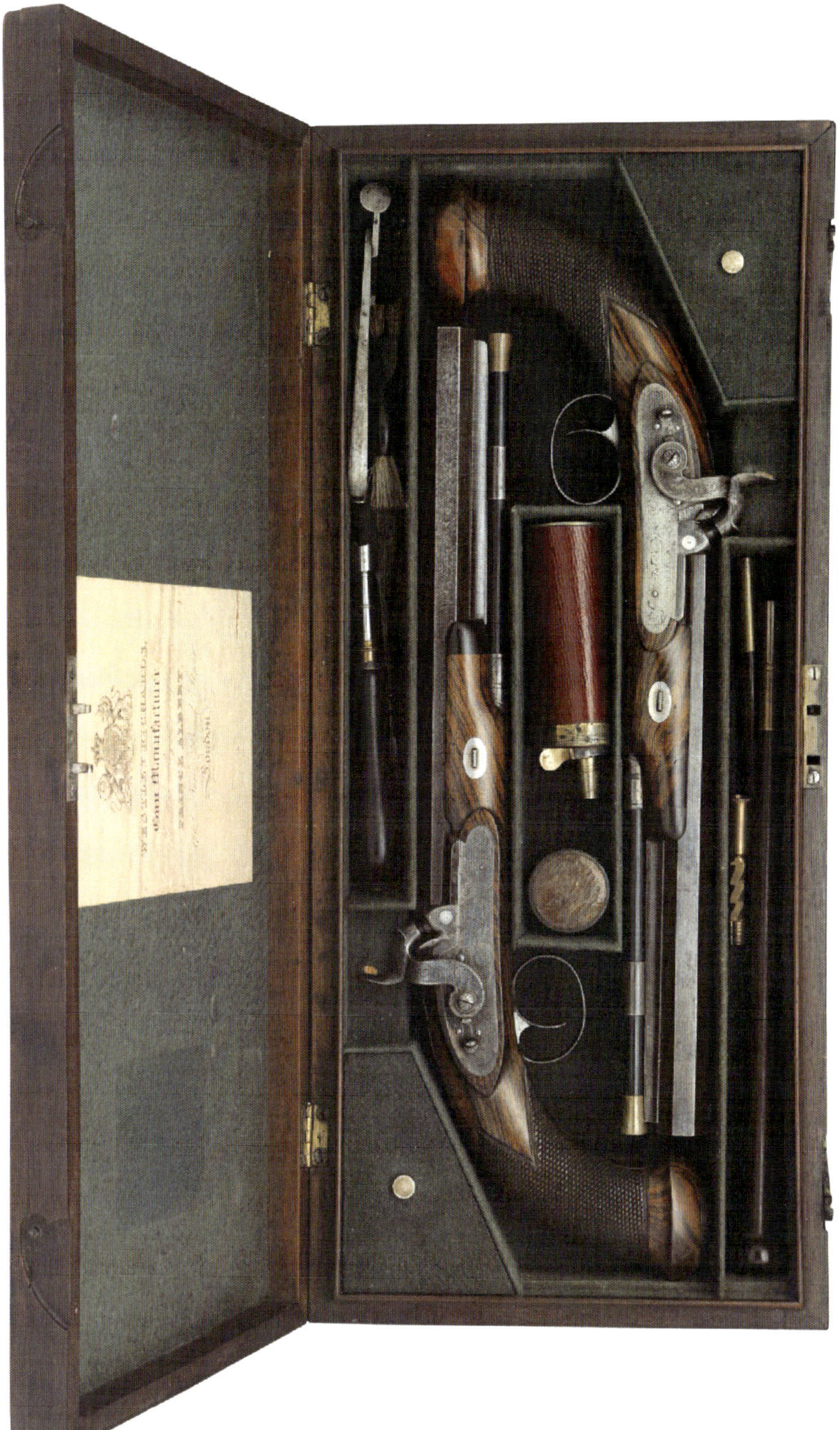

Figure 36:
An extremely late pair of 28 bore pistols, circa 1867-1876,
by a London maker John Blissett and Sons.

Dating from the very end of duelling in Britain these pistols are
so similar to the Continental examples. The half-stocks, with typical
butts, have no provision for a fitted ramrod but have blued steel
furniture. The mahogany case has a special section to house wads
used to ensure a particularly tight fit for the ball.

Figure 37:
These pistols dating from around 1776-1780 are by the
London maker John Twigg.

They show signs of a gradual change of the general pattern to
the duelling pistol with 25 bore barrels, stepped lock but no safety
catches. The walnut stocks still have some simple decoration.

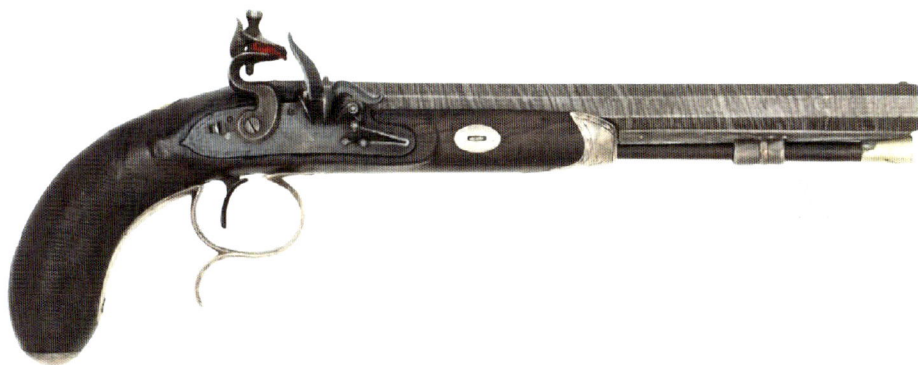

Figure 38
Single pistol by T. Pattison of Dublin dated 1803
and numbered 167.

There are signs that it may have been converted from flint to percussion and back again. It still has early features such as a small butt cap but also the newer spurred trigger guard and platinum plug.

Figure 39:
A pair by John Manton & Son of Dover Street London,
numbered 11175 and dating from around 1840-1844.

In many ways they are Continental in style with half stock without provision for a ramrod but the butts are still traditional with chequering, stocks with blued steel trigger guard with stylized pineapple finial. The mahogany case holds accessories including three way flask, a bullet mould, combination T shaped tool and a combined rammer with mallet head.